P9-ARL-030

THE MULTICULTURAL EDUCATION DIRECTORY

THE MULTICULTURAL EDUCATION DIRECTORY

DAVID E. WASHBURN
& NEIL L. BROWN

Philadelphia

Produced, Edited, and Designed by DANIEL C. WASHBURN

Printed in the United States of America.

Library of Congress Catalog Number 96-77220

ISBN 0-9635521-3-9

Inquiry International
Business Office, 7015 Scenic Drive, Bloomsburg, PA 17815
Editorial Office, 1203 Brighton Street, Philadelphia, PA 19111

This book is printed on acid-free paper.

To Faith G. Kline, fourth grade teacher at the John L. Kinsey Elementary School in Philadelphia, Pennsylvania, Kathy Brown, first grade teacher at the Marvine Elementary School in Bethlehem, Pennsylvania, and all those other teachers who, on a daily basis, expend every fiber of their beings in an effort to reach, teach, and nurture the children of the United States of America.

Contents

Preface

This comprehensive, state by state study of multicultural education programs in the United States contains a detailed listing of every large school district's multicultural education program, including: years in operation, grade levels included, number of students involved, degree of community involvement, social goals, school goals, primary target population, curricular aims, instructional aims, classroom environment, school practices, materials produced and their availability for purchase. Every aspect of each district's program is cross-referenced and listed in Chapter One through Chapter Nine for easy use. This book also features a listing of all districts with ethnic studies programs (included in Chapter One) and in-depth descriptions of their curriculum, groups studied, and disciplines participating. In Chapter Ten, each district is listed by state with program contact persons, addresses, phone numbers, and a complete program description.

Most of the material herein contained is self-explanatory. When it comes to designations of *social goals*, *school goals*, *curricular aims*, *instructional aims*, and *classroom environment*, we use shorthand designations based on a typology developed by Christine E. Sleeter and Carl A. Grant. Sleeter and Grant[1] have provided a useful typology of conceptions of multicultural education breaking schooling down to *business as usual* and five approaches to multicultural education: *teaching the exceptional and culturally different*, *human relations*, *single-group studies*, *multicultural education*, and *education that is multicultural and social reconstructionist.* Since their analysis has been influential in providing a framework for investigation of multicultural education and many in the field are familiar with their typology, their designations are utilized in this directory.

According to the Sleeter and Grant typology *business as usual* is traditional, teacher-centered education with little accommodation to differing student learning styles or individualization. Teachers utilizing this approach focus their attention on the white, male, and middle-class students more than others in the same classroom. The curriculum is Euro-centric in spite of the availability of materials which reflect cultural diversity. Neighborhood schools tend to be unidimensional in terms of ethnicity and social class. Grouping and tracking in more heterogeneous settings resegregates students along racial, ethnic, gender, and social class lines. Students in the different tracks and groups are treated differently with lower expectations being maintained for ethnic minority students. In general the patterns in the business as usual settings mirror and reproduce the race, social class, and gender patterns of the broader society.[2]

Schools operating from the *teaching the exceptional and culturally different* approach try to fit students into the existing social structure and culture. They teach lower-class, minority, special education, limited-English proficiency, or female students who are behind in the main school subjects' traditional subject matter by building on students' learning styles and adapting to their skill levels. They attempt to make traditional subject matter relevant to students' experiential backgrounds. The focus is on integration of the exceptional and culturally different students into mainstream society by involving their parents in supporting the work of the school and using transitional bilingual education, English as a second language, remedial classes, and special education to this end.[3]

The societal goal of those advocating the *human relations* approach is to promote feelings of unity, tolerance, and acceptance among people within the existing social structure. In school they try to promote positive feelings among all students by reducing stereotyping and to enhance students' self-concepts. They utilize cooperative learning and student experiences in teaching lessons about stereotyping, individual differences, and the contributions to society made by members of various groups. In general, this orientation promotes classroom and school themes which promote general human welfare.[4]

Single-group studies promote social structural equality for and immediate recognition of the identified group. They call on all students to work for change that would benefit a particular group. They employ faculty who are group members and utilize the learning style of the group in teaching about the group, their history of victimization, and current issues involving the group from the group's point of view. Classrooms are decorated to reflect the group. Representatives of the group are asked to become involved in class activities as guest speakers and resource persons.[5]

According to Sleeter and Grant, advocates of *multicultural education* wish to promote social structural equality and cultural pluralism in the society and equal opportunity, cultural pluralism, respect for cultural and lifestyle differences, and support of power equity among groups in the school. The general curriculum for all students is organized around the contribution and perspectives of various cultural groups and utilizes the students' experiential backgrounds and learning styles in promoting bilingualism and multilingualism, and critical analyses of alternative viewpoints. Teachers actively involve students in thinking and analyzing through the use of cooperative learning and other instructional strategies. A diversity focus is evident in classroom decorations, support services, involvement of parents and community members, school menus, library materials, staffing patterns, extracurricular activities, and accessibility of the building.[6]

The approach favored by Sleeter and Grant is education that is *multicultural and social reconstructionist.* They wish to promote social structural equality and cultural pluralism in the society by preparing citizens to work actively toward these goals through education. Therefore, all school children should be taught by a curriculum organized around current social issues involving racism, classism, sexism, and handicapism. They advocate the organization of concepts around experiences and perspectives of several different American groups; use students' life experiences as starting points for analyzing oppression; teach critical thinking skills, analysis of alternative viewpoints, and social action and empowerment skills. They suggest that students should be actively involved in democratic decision-making; instruction should accommodate to diverse learning styles and skill levels through cooperative learning; social action themes should dominate the classroom; testing and grouping which designates some students as failures should be avoided; respect for cultural diversity should be the focus of the school's staffing patterns, school menus, library materials, extracurricular activities, building accessibility, discipline procedures, and support services; and involvement of students, parents, and community members in democratic decision-making about substantive school-wide concerns.[7]

Following are the questions asked of each school district followed by the Sleeter and Grant designation:

Which one of the following comes closest to characterizing the *social goal* of you multicultural education program?

- help students fit into present society (*teaching the exceptional and culturally different*)
- promote tolerance and acceptance within present society (*human relations*)
- promote equality and recognition of a particular group or groups (*single-group studies*)
- promote social equality and cultural pluralism (*multicultural education*)
- promote active change which will enhance the power position of oppressed peoples (*education that is multicultural and social reconstructionist*)

Which one of the following comes closest to characterizing the *school goals* of your multicultural education program?

- teach students to become culturally literate by making the core disciplines relevant to their lives (*teaching the exceptional and culturally different*)
- promote positive feelings among students, reduce stereotyping, promote students' self-concepts (*human relations*)
- develop in students the motivation and knowledge to work toward social change that would benefit their particular group (*single-group studies*)

- promote equal opportunity in the school, cultural pluralism, respect for those who differ, and support of power equality among groups (*multicultural education*)
- prepare citizens to work actively toward social equality; promote cultural pluralism and alternative lifestyles; promote equal opportunity in the school (*education that is multicultural and social reconstructionist*)

Which one set of practices comes closest to characterizing the *curricular aims* of your multicultural education program?

- make the curriculum relevant to students' experiential background; fill in gaps in basic skills and knowledge (*teaching the exceptional and culturally different*)
- teach lessons about stereotyping, name-calling, individual differences and similarities, and contributions of groups of which students are members (*human relations*)
- teach units or courses about the culture of a group, how the group has been victimized, current social issues facing the group—from the perspective of that group (*single-group studies*)
- teach contributions and perspectives of several different groups, critical thinking, analyses of alternative viewpoints; make curriculum relevant to students' experiential backgrounds; promote use of more than one language or dialect (*multicultural education*)
- teach current social issues involving racism, classism, sexism, handicapism; teach experiences and perspectives of several different American groups; use students' life experiences as a starting point for analyzing oppression; teach critical thinking, analysis of alternative viewpoints, social action and empowerment (*education that is multicultural and social reconstructionist*)

Which one of the following comes closest to characterizing the *instructional aims* of your multicultural education program?

- build on students' learning styles; adapt to students' skill levels; teach as effectively and efficiently as possible to enable students to catch up (*teaching the exceptional and culturally different*)
- use cooperative learning; use real or vicarious experiences with others (*human relations*)

- build on the learning styles of the students' groups (*single-group studies*)
- build on the students' learning styles; adapt to the students' skill levels; involve students actively in thinking and analyzing; use cooperative learning (*multicultural education*)
- involve students actively in democratic decision making; build on students' learning styles; adapt to students' skill levels; use cooperative learning; develop a spirit of social activism (*education that is multicultural and social reconstructionist*)

Which of the following *aspects of the classroom* are incorporated into your multicultural education program?

- use decorations showing group members integrated into mainstream of society (*teaching the exceptional and culturally different*)
- decorate classroom to reflect uniqueness and accomplishments of students; decorate in "I'm okay, you're okay" themes (*human relations*)
- use decorations reflecting cultural and classroom contributions of a particular group; have representatives of a particular group involved in class (e.g. as guest speakers) (*single-group studies*)
- decorate classroom to reflect cultural pluralism, nontraditional sex roles, disabled people, and student interests (*multicultural education*)
- decorate classroom to reflect social action themes, cultural diversity, student interests, and aspects of society that need to be changed in order to achieve equal justice for all (*education that is multicultural and social reconstructionist*)

NOTES

1. Christine E. Sleeter and Carl A. Grant, *Making Choices for Multicultural Education: Five Approaches to Race, Class, and Gender* (Columbus: Merril Publishing Company, 1988).
2. *Ibid.*, 14-26.
3. *Ibid.*, 67.
5. *Ibid.*, 100.
6. *Ibid.*, 131.
7. *Ibid.*, 201.

Chapter One

Multicultural Education Programs by State

MULTICULTURAL EDUCATION PROGRAMS BY STATE

• denotes programs which include an ethnic studies curriculum

Chapter Two

Groups Studied in Ethnic Studies Curricula

AFRICAN AMERICANS

ASIAN/PACIFIC ISLANDER AMERICANS

Haitian Americans

Hispanic (Latino/Chicano) Americans

Scandinavian Americans

California	Conejo Valley Unified 122
	Norwalk-La Mirada Unified 132
	San Diego City Unified 134
Connecticut	Hartford 142
Florida	Duval County 148
Georgia	Cobb County 157
Minnesota	Duluth 189
New Jersey	Jersey City 202
Tennessee	Hamilton County 232
Utah	Weber 247
Virginia	Portsmouth City 249
Washington	Bethel 252
	Renton 256

Slavic Americans

California	Conejo Valley Unified 122
	Norwalk-La Mirada Unified 132
	San Diego City Unified 134
Connecticut	Hartford 142
Florida	Duval County 148
	Sarasota County 154
Georgia	Cobb County 157
Indiana	Perry Township 165
Minnesota	Duluth 189
New Jersey	Jersey City 202
	Trenton City 203
Tennessee	Hamilton County 232
Utah	Weber 247
Washington	Bethel 252
	Renton 256

Chapter Three

Disciplines Participating in Ethnic Studies Curricula

ART

BUSINESS

FOREIGN LANGUAGES

HEALTH

HOME ECONOMICS

HUMANITIES

Arkansas	Fort Smith (Compensatory) 117
California	Capistrano Unified 121
	Clovis Unified 121
	Conejo Valley Unified 122
	Fremont Unified 125
	Los Angeles Unified 129
	Norwalk-La Mirada Unified 132
	Oxnard Union High 133
	San Diego City Unified 134
	San Francisco Unified 135
	Ventura Unified 137
Colorado	Denver County 139
Florida	Collier County 147
	Dade County 147
	Duval County 148
	Escambia County 149
	Hillsborough County 149
	Saint Lucie County 153
Georgia	Bibb County 155
	Cobb County 157
	De Kalb County 159
Indiana	New Albany-Floyd County 164
Iowa	Siuox City Community 169
Maryland	Wicomico County 178
Massachusetts	Fall River 180
	New Bedford 181
	Springfield 182
Michigan	Dearborn City 183
	Lansing 185
Minnesota	Duluth 189
Missouri	Columbia 193
	Lee's Summit 195
	St. Joseph 197
	St. Louis City 197
Nebraska	Lincoln 198
	Omaha 199
New Jersey	Elizabeth City 201
	Jersey City 202
	Paterson City 203
New Mexico	Albuquerque 204
	Las Cruces 206
	Santa Fe 206
North Carolina	Cabarrus County 211
Ohio	Akron City 216
	Dayton City 218
	Springfield City 219
Oklahoma	Edmond 221
	Oklahoma City 222
	Tulsa 223
Oregon	Portland 225

SCIENCE

Chapter Four

Elements Studied in Ethnic Studies Curricula

ART

State	School District	Page
Alabama	Baldwin County	110
Alaska	Anchorage	111
	Fairbanks North Star Boro	112
Arizona	Roosevelt	115
Arkansas	Fort Smith (Compensatory)	117
	Little Rock	117
California	Anaheim Union High	118
	Capistrano Unified	121
	Clovis Unified	121
	Conejo Valley Unified	122
	Fremont Unified	125
	Fresno Unified	125
	Los Angeles Unified	129
	Norwalk-La Mirada Unified	132
	Oxnard Union High	133
	San Diego City Unified	134
	San Francisco Unified	135
	San Juan Unified	136
	Ventura Unified	137
Colorado	Adams-Arapahoe	138
	Denver County	139
	Mesa County Valley	140
Connecticut	Hartford	142
Florida	Brevard County	145
	Broward County	146
	Collier County	147
	Dade County	147
	Escambia County	149
	Okaloosa County	151
Georgia	Bibb County	155
	Carroll County	156
	Cobb County	157
	De Kalb County	159
Illinois	East St. Louis	161
Indiana	New Albany-Floyd County	164
Iowa	Des Moines Independent	168
	Siuox City Community	169
Kansas	Olathe	170
Kentucky	Hardin County	172
Maryland	Saint Mary's County	177
	Wicomico County	178
Massachusetts	Fall River	180
	New Bedford	181
	Springfield	182
	Worcester	183
Michigan	Dearborn City	183
	Lansing	185

ATTITUDES

BELIEFS

CULTURE AND PERSONALITY

FOODS

HISTORY

LANGUAGE

MUSIC

PHYSICAL CHARACTERISTICS

SOCIAL CUSTOMS

SOCIAL ORGANIZATION

SOCIAL STRUCTURE

VALUES

Chapter Five

Social Goals for Multicultural Education Programs

TEACHING THE EXCEPTIONAL AND CULTURALLY DIFFERENT

HUMAN RELATIONS

Single-Group Studies

Multicultural Education

Georgia	Cobb County	157
Indiana	New Albany-Floyd County	164
	Wayne Township	166
Massachusetts	Springfield	182
Nebraska	Lincoln	198
New York	Syracuse City	208
Pennsylvania	Philadelphia City	227
Washington	Vancouver	258
Wisconsin	Madison Metropolitan	262

Chapter Six

School Goals for Multicultural Education Programs

TEACHING THE EXCEPTIONAL AND CULTURALLY DIFFERENT

State	*School District*	*Page*
Alabama	Baldwin County	110
Arizona	Tucson Unified	116
California	Folsom-Cordova Unified	123
	Mt. Diablo Unified	131
	Oceanside City Unified	133
	Saddleback Valley Unified	134
Connecticut	Hartford	142
Florida	Broward County	146
	Osceola County	152
Kentucky	Boone County	171
Maryland	Carroll County	175
	Washington County	178
Michigan	Saginaw	186
Minnesota	Rosemount	191
New Hampshire	Manchester	200
New Mexico	Gallup-McKinley County	205
New York	Sachem	207
North Carolina	Gaston County	212
	New Hanover County	213
	Randolph County	214
Ohio	Akron City	216
	Cleveland City	217
Oklahoma	Putnam	223
Oregon	Portland	225
South Carolina	Pickens County	231
	Richland	231
Texas	Midland	243
	Northside	244
Virginia	Prince William County	250
	Richmond City	250
West Virginia	Berkeley County	259

HUMAN RELATIONS

State	School District	Page
Alabama	Mobile County	111
Arizona	Cartwright	112
	Deer Valley Unified	113
	Paradise Valley	113
	Peoria Unified	114
	Pheonix Unified	114
California	Antelope Valley Union High	119
	Burbank Unified	120
	Conejo Valley Unified	122
	Fresno Unified	125
	Glendale Unified	126
	Grossmont Union High	127
	Inglewood Unified	128
	Modesto City Elementary	130
	Modesto City High	130

	San Juan Unified	136
	Santa Ana Unified	136
	Simi Valley Unified	137
	Ventura Unified	137
Florida	Brevard County	145
	Charlotte County	146
	Dade County	147
	Duval County	148
	Okaloosa County	151
	Orange County	151
	Pasco County	152
	Sarasota County	154
	Volusia County	154
Georgia	Bibb County	155
	Coweta County	158
Illinois	East St. Louis	161
	Naperville	161
	Springfield	162
Indiana	Monroe County	164
	Perry Township	165
	South Bend Community	165
Kansas	Olathe	170
Kentucky	Hardin County	172
Louisiana	Iberia Parish	172
Maryland	Anne Arundel County	174
	Calvert County	175
Massachusetts	New Bedford	181
Michigan	Detroit	184
	Traverse City	187
	Wayne-Westland	188
Minnesota	Bloomington	188
Missouri	Columbia	193
	Independence	194
	Lee's Summit	195
	Rockwood	196
Nevada	Washoe County	200
New Jersey	Edison	201
	Elizabeth City	201
North Carolina	Alamance County	210
	Catawba County	211
	Craven County	212
North Dakota	Bismark	215
	Fargo	215
Ohio	Dayton City	218
	Lakota	218
	Toledo City	220
Oklahoma	Edmond	221
	Oklahoma City	222
	Tulsa	223
Oregon	Bend/Lapine	224

EDUCATION THAT IS MULTICULTURAL AND SOCIAL RECONSTRUCTIONIST

Chapter Seven

Curricular Aims of Multicultural Education Programs

TEACHING THE EXCEPTIONAL AND CULTURALLY DIFFERENT

State	*School District*	*Page*
Alabama	Mobile County	111
California	Burbank Unified	120
	Modesto City Elementary	130
	Mt. Diablo Unified	131
	Norwalk-La Mirada Unified	132
	Saddleback Valley Unified	134
Florida	Charlotte County	146
Georgia	Coweta County	158
	De Kalb County	159
Idaho	Idaho Falls	160
Illinois	Springfield	162
Kentucky	Boone County	171
Michigan	Rochester Community	186
	Saginaw	186
	Walled Lake	187
New Jersey	Edison	201
	Elizabeth City	201
New Mexico	Las Cruces	206
	Santa Fe	206
North Carolina	Alamance County	210
	Burke County	210
	Gaston County	212
North Dakota	Fargo	215
Ohio	Cincinnati City	216
Oklahoma	Moore	221
Oregon	Bend/Lapine	224
South Carolina	Pickens County	231
	Richland	231
South Dakota	Rapid City	232
Tennessee	Sumner County	234
Utah	Alpine	245
	Jordan	246
Virginia	Portsmouth City	249
	Prince William County	250
Washington	Bethel	252
	Clover Park	253
	Yakima	259

HUMAN RELATIONS

Arizona	Deer Valley Unified	113
	Paradise Valley	113
California	Antelope Valley Union High	119
	Modesto City High	130
Florida	Brevard County	145
Illinois	East St. Louis	161
Indiana	South Bend Community	165
Kansas	Olathe	170
	Wichita	171

Maryland	Carroll County	175
Massachusetts	Fall River	180
	New Bedford	181
Missouri	Columbia	193
	Independence	194
Nevada	Washoe County	200
North Carolina	Catawba County	211
	Nash County	213
Ohio	Toledo City	220
Oklahoma	Oklahoma City	222
Pennsylvania	Bethlehem	226
South Carolina	Charleston County	230
	Horry County	230
Tennessee	Shelby County	233
Texas	Arlington	236
	Deer Park	238
	Houston	241
	Midland	243
Washington	Tacoma	258

Single-Group Studies

California	Ventura Unified	137
Florida	Osceola County	152
	Saint Lucie County	153
Michigan	Wayne-Westland	188
Missouri	Lee's Summit	195
Ohio	Worthington City	220
Oklahoma	Edmond	221
	Tulsa	223
Texas	Northside	244
West Virginia	Harrison County	260
Wisconsin	Eau Claire	261

Multicultural Education

Alabama	Baldwin County	110
Alaska	Fairbanks North Star Boro	112
Arizona	Cartwright	112
	Peoria Unified	114
	Roosevelt	115
	Scottsdale Unified	115
	Tucson Unified	116
Arkansas	Little Rock	117
California	Bellflower Unified	120
	East Side Union High	123
	Folsom-Cordova Unified	123
	Fresno Unified	125
	Glendale Unified	126
	Grant Joint Union High	127
	Grossmont Union High	127
	Inglewood Unified	128
	Napa Valley Unified	131

EDUCATION THAT IS MULTICULTURAL AND SOCIAL RECONSTRUCTIONIST

Chapter Eight

Instructional Aims of Multicultural Education Programs

Teaching the Exceptional and Culturally Different

Human Relations

Single-Group Studies

MULTICULTURAL EDUCATION

EDUCATION THAT IS MULTICULTURAL AND SOCIAL RECONSTRUCTIONIST

Chapter Nine

Multicultural Education Programs with Locally Produced Materials Available for Purchase

School Districts with Locally Produced Multicultural Education Materials Available for Purchase

Chapter Ten

Multicultural Education Program Descriptions

ALABAMA

BALDWIN COUNTY
Barbara H. Brown
175 Courthouse Square
Bay Minette, AL 36507
(334) 990-2237

Years In Operation: 6; **Grade Levels:** K-12; **Students Participating:** 13,000; **Community Participation:** use of community resources, use of human resources in the community, study of the community, interaction with community organizations; **Social Goal:** human relations; **School Goal:** teaching the culturally different; **Primary Target:** all students; **Curricular Aims:** multicultural education; **Instructional Aims:** multicultural education; **Classroom Environment:** single-group studies; **School Practices:** ESL, human relations training for teachers, strong school-community public relations effort, inservice teacher training in multicultural education, student involvement in curriculum planning, Spanish as a second language, interracial student council, professionally staffed community relations office, ethnic studies curriculum; **Groups Studied:** African Americans, Asian/Pacific Islander Americans, French Americans, German Americans, Hispanic (Latino/Chicano) Americans, Italian Americans, Native Americans; **Elements Studied:** art, beliefs, culture and personality, foods, history, language, literature, music, religion, social customs; **Participating Disciplines:** art, foreign languages, humanities, language arts, music, reading, social studies; **Locally Produced Materials:** yes.

JEFFERSON COUNTY
Nancy Sargent
Division Superintendent for Curriculum & Instruction
1800 21st Street
Birmingham, AL 35209
(205) 325-5207

Years In Operation: 1; **Grade Levels:** K-12; **Students Participating:** 40,598; **Community Involvement:** community involvement in curriculum planning; **Classroom Environment:** multicultural education; **School Practices:** remedial classes, culturally diverse faculty, interracial student council, human relations training for students, bilingual curriculum, student human relations council.

Mobile County
Maggie G. Rivers
Supervisor
P.O. Box 1327
Mobile, AL 36633
(205) 690-8250

Years In Operation: 10; **Grade Levels:** K-12; **Students Participating:** 330; **Community Participation:** interaction with community organizations, quarterly parent training workshops; **Social Goal:** teaching the culturally different; **School Goal:** human relations; **Primary Target:** all students; **Curricular Aims:** teaching the culturally different; **Instructional Aims:** multicultural education; **Classroom Environment:** multicultural education; **School Practices:** ESL, culturally diverse faculty, culturally diverse staff, human relations training for teachers, community involvement in school policy decisions, inservice teacher training in multicultural education, interracial student council; **Locally Produced Materials:** yes.

ALASKA

Anchorage
Maxine Hill
Supervisor
P.O. Box 196614
Anchorage, AK 99519
(907) 269-2284

Years In Operation: 16; **Grade Levels:** K-12; **Students Participating:** 47,560; **Community Participation:** community involvement in curriculum planning, use of community resources, use of human resources in the community; **Social Goal:** multicultural education; **School Goal:** multicultural/social reconstructionist; **Primary Target:** all students; **Curricular Aims:** multicultural/social reconstructionist; **Instructional Aims:** multicultural/social reconstructionist; **Classroom Environment:** multicultural/social reconstructionist; **School Practices:** transitional bilingual education, ESL, remedial classes, culturally diverse faculty, parental involvement in school policy decisions, culturally diverse staff, human relations training for teachers, community involvement in school policy decisions, strong school-community public relations effort, inservice teacher training in multicultural education, student involvement in curriculum planning, Spanish as a second language, student involvement in school policy decisions, interracial student council, human relations training for students, bilingual curriculum, professionally staffed human relations team, bicultural curriculum, standard English as a second dialect, Asian language(s), ethnic studies curriculum; **Groups Studied:** African Americans, Native Americans; **Elements Studied:** art, beliefs, body language, culture and personality, history, language, literature, music, social customs, social organization, values; **Participating Disciplines:** language arts, music, reading, social studies

FAIRBANKS NORTH STAR BORO
Chris Hill
Alaskan Native Education
Cynthia Terres
Bilingual/Bicultural Program
520 Fifth Avenue
Fairbanks, AK 99707
(907) 452-2000

Years In Operation: 11; **Grade Levels:** K-12; **Students Participating:** 4,500; **Community Participation:** community involvement in curriculum planning, use of community resources, use of human resources in the community, a community based instructional program, study of the community, interaction with community organizations; **Social Goal:** multicultural education; **School Goal:** multicultural education; **Primary Target:** all students; **Curricular Aims:** multicultural education; **Instructional Aims:** multicultural education; **Classroom Environment:** multicultural education; **School Practices:** transitional bilingual education, ESL, remedial classes, culturally diverse faculty, parental involvement in school policy decisions, culturally diverse staff, strong school-community public relations effort, inservice teacher training in multicultural education, Spanish as a second language, student human relations council, standard English as a second dialect, Native American language(s), ethnic studies curriculum; **Group Studied:** Native Americans; **Elements Studied:** art, attitudes, beliefs, culture and personality, dialect, foods, history, kinship structure, language, literature, material culture, music, social customs, social organization, social structure, values; **Participating Disciplines:** art, language arts, music, physical education, social studies; **Locally Produced Materials:** yes; **Materials Available for Purchase:** yes.

ARIZONA

CARTWRIGHT
Assistant Superintendent
3402 North 67th Avenue
Phoenix, AZ 85033
(602) 846-2800

Years In Operation: 3; **Grade Levels:** K-8; **Students Participating:** 16,000; **Community Participation:** use of community resources, use of human resources in the community; **Social Goal:** human relations; **School Goal:** human relations; **Primary Target:** all students; **Curricular Aims:** multicultural education; **Instructional Aims:** multicultural education; **Classroom Environment:** multicultural/social reconstructionist; **School Practices:** transitional bilingual education, ESL, remedial classes, culturally diverse faculty, parental involvement in school policy decisions, human relations training for teachers, inservice teacher training in multicultural education, Spanish as a second language, bilingual curriculum; **Elements Studied:** art, beliefs, drama, foods, history, kinship structure, language, literature, music, religion, social customs, values; **Participating Disciplines:** art, English, foreign languages, health, humanities, language arts, mathematics, music, reading, science, social studies, theater.

Deer Valley Unified
Lloyd R. Gillum
Student Development Coordinator
20402 North 15th Avenue
Phoenix, AZ 85027
(602) 581-7814

Years In Operation: 6; **Grade Levels:** K-12; **Students Participating:** 20,000; **Community Participation:** use of human resources in the community, interaction with community organizations; **Social Goal:** human relations; **School Goal:** human relations; **Primary Target:** all students; **Curricular Aims:** human relations; **Instructional Aims:** multicultural education; **Classroom Environment:** multicultural education; **School Practices:** ESL, remedial classes, culturally diverse faculty, parental involvement in school policy decisions, culturally diverse staff, community involvement in school policy decisions, strong school-community public relations effort, human relations training for students, professionally staffed community relations office, standard English as a second dialect; **Elements Studied:** art, foods, history, music.

Paradise Valley
Toby Spessard
Assistant Superintendent
15002 North 32nd Street
Phoenix, AZ 85032
(602) 867-5728

Years In Operation: 4; **Grade Levels:** K-12; **Students Participating:** 32,000; **Community Participation:** use of community resources, use of human resources in the community, interaction with community organizations, human relations task force; **Social Goal:** multicultural education; **School Goal:** human relations; **Primary Target:** all students; **Curricular Aims:** human relations; **Instructional Aims:** multicultural/social reconstructionist; **Classroom Environment:** multicultural/social reconstructionist; **School Practices:** ESL, remedial classes, culturally diverse faculty, parental involvement in school policy decisions, human relations training for teachers, community involvement in school policy decisions, strong school-community public relations effort, inservice teacher training in multicultural education, student involvement in school policy decisions, interracial student council, human relations training for students, professionally staffed community relations office, professionally staffed human relations team.

PEORIA UNIFIED
Barbara Volk
6330 West Thunderbird
Glendale, AZ 85306
(602) 486-6066

Years In Operation: 11; **Grade Levels:** K-12; **Students Participating:** 25,600; **Community Participation:** use of community resources, use of human resources in the community, study of the community, interaction with community organizations; **Social Goal:** human relations; **School Goal:** human relations; **Primary Target:** all students; **Curricular Aims:** multicultural education; **Instructional Aims:** multicultural/social reconstructionist; **Classroom Environment:** multicultural/social reconstructionist; **School Practices:** transitional bilingual education, ESL, remedial classes, culturally diverse faculty, parental involvement in school policy decisions, culturally diverse staff, community involvement in school policy decisions, strong school-community public relations effort, inservice teacher training in multicultural education, Spanish as a second language, student involvement in school policy decisions, interracial student council, human relations training for students, professionally staffed community relations office, bilingual curriculum, professionally staffed human relations team, student human relations council, bicultural curriculum, Asian language(s).

PHOENIX UNIFIED
Dr. Josephine Pete
4502 North Central Ave.
Phoenix, AZ 85012
(602) 271-3100

Years In Operation: 5; **Grade Levels:** 9-12; **Community Participation:** use of community resources, use of human resources in the community, a community based instructional program, interaction with community organizations; **Social Goal:** multicultural education; **School Goal:** human relations; **Primary Target:** all students; **Curricular Aims:** multicultural/social reconstructionist; **Instructional Aims:** multicultural education; **Classroom Environment:** multicultural/social reconstructionist; **School Practices:** ESL, remedial classes, culturally diverse faculty, culturally diverse staff, human relations training for teachers, community involvement in school policy decisions, strong school-community public relations effort, inservice teacher training in multicultural education, Spanish as a second language, student involvement in school policy decisions, human relations training for students, professionally staffed community relations office, bilingual curriculum, professionally staffed human relations team, bicultural curriculum, multilingual curriculum, standard English as a second dialect, Asian language(s), ethnic studies curriculum; **Groups Studied:** African Americans, Asian/Pacific Islander Americans, French Americans, German Americans, Hispanic (Latino/Chicano) Americans, Native Americans; **Participating Disciplines:** art, English, humanities, language arts, social studies; **Locally Produced Materials:** yes.

Roosevelt
Clementina Montiel-Salinas
Multicultural & Curriculum Director
6000 South 7th Street
Phoenix, AZ 85040
(602) 243-4800

Years In Operation: 1; **Grade Levels:** K-8; **Students Participating:** 11,500; **Community Participation:** use of community resources, use of human resources in the community, interaction with community organizations; **Social Goal:** multicultural education; **School Goal:** multicultural/social reconstructionist; **Primary Target:** all students; **Curricular Aims:** multicultural education; **Instructional Aims:** multicultural education; **Classroom Environment:** multicultural/social reconstructionist; **School Practices:** transitional bilingual education, ESL, parental involvement in school policy decisions, culturally diverse staff, community involvement in school policy decisions, strong school-community public relations effort, student involvement in curriculum planning, Spanish as a second language, student involvement in school policy decisions, interracial student council, bilingual curriculum, multilingual curriculum, ethnic studies curriculum; **Groups Studied:** African Americans, Hispanic (Latino/Chicano) Americans; **Elements Studied:** art, foods, literature, material culture, music, social customs, values; **Participating Disciplines:** art, foreign languages, language arts, music, social studies.

Scottsdale Unified
3811 North 44th St.
Phoenix, AZ 85018
(602) 952-6100

Years In Operation: 8; **Grade Levels:** K-12; **Students Participating:** 10,000; **Community Participation:** community involvement in curriculum planning, use of community resources, use of human resources in the community, interaction with community organizations; **Social Goal:** single-group studies; **School Goal:** multicultural education; **Primary Target:** all students; **Curricular Aims:** multicultural education; **Instructional Aims:** multicultural/social reconstructionist; **Classroom Environment:** multicultural/social reconstructionist; **School Practices:** ESL, remedial classes, culturally diverse faculty, parental involvement in school policy decisions, culturally diverse staff, human relations training for teachers, community involvement in school policy decisions, strong school-community public relations effort, inservice teacher training in multicultural education, student involvement in curriculum planning, Spanish as a second language, student involvement in school policy decisions, interracial student council, human relations training for students, professionally staffed community relations office, Asian language(s); **Locally Produced Materials:** yes; **Materials Available for Purchase:** yes.

Tempe Elementary
Lucy Urias
Supervisor, Language & Multicultural Education
3205 South Rural Road
Tempe, AZ 85285
(602) 730-7219

Tuscon Unified
Tommy Harper
Director of Curriculum
442 East 7th Street
Tuscon, AZ 85717
(602) 882-2400

Years In Operation: 5; **Grade Levels:** K-12; **Students Participating:** 63,000; **Community Participation:** community involvement in curriculum planning, use of community resources, use of human resources in the community, a community based instructional program, study of the community, interaction with community organizations; **Social Goal:** multicultural education; **School Goal:** teaching the culturally different; **Primary Target:** all students; **Curricular Aims:** multicultural education; **Instructional Aims:** multicultural education; **Classroom Environment:** multicultural/social reconstructionist; **School Practices:** transitional bilingual education, ESL, culturally diverse faculty, culturally diverse staff, human relations training for teachers, community involvement in school policy decisions, inservice teacher training in multicultural education, student involvement in curriculum planning, Spanish as a second language, student involvement in school policy decisions, human relations training for students, bilingual curriculum, bicultural curriculum, multilingual curriculum; **Locally Produced Materials:** yes; **Materials Available for Purchase:** yes.

ARKANSAS

Fort Smith
Judy Story
Supervisor of Title V, ESL, & Migrant Education
P.O. Box 1948
Fort Smith, AR 72902
(501) 785-2501

Years In Operation: 20; **Grade Levels:** K-12; **Students Participating:** 650; **Community Participation:** use of community resources, use of human resources in the community, study of the community, interaction with community organizations, Volunteers in Education, Partners in Education; **Social Goal:** multicultural education; **School Goal:** multicultural education; **Primary Target:** minority students; **Curricular Aims:** multicultural/social reconstructionist; **Instructional Aims:** multicultural education; **Classroom Environment:** multicultural education; **School Practices:** transitional bilingual education, ESL, culturally diverse faculty, parental involvement in school policy decisions, community involvement in school policy decisions, strong school-community public relations effort, inservice teacher training in multicultural education, student involvement in curriculum planning, Spanish as a second language, interracial student council, human relations training for students.

Fort Smith
Marc Soucy
Director of Compensatory Education
P.O. Box 1948
Fort Smith, AR 72902
(501) 785-2501

Years In Operation: 10; **Grade Levels:** K-12; **Students Participating:** 12,500; **Community Participation:** use of human resources in the community; **Social Goal:** human relations; **School Goal:** multicultural education; **Primary Target:** all students; **Curricular Aims:** multicultural/social reconstructionist; **Instructional Aims:** multicultural education; **Classroom Environment:** multicultural/social reconstructionist; **School Practices:** transitional bilingual education, ESL, remedial classes, culturally diverse faculty, parental involvement in school policy decisions, human relations training for teachers, community involvement in school policy decisions, strong school-community public relations effort, inservice teacher training in multicultural education, ethnic studies curriculum; **Groups Studied:** African Americans, Asian/Pacific Islander Americans, Hispanic (Latino/Chicano) Americans, Native Americans; **Elements Studied:** art, beliefs, body language, foods, kinship structure, music, social customs; **Participating Disciplines:** art, foreign languages, language arts, music, reading, social studies.

Little Rock
Marie McNeal
Supervisor of Social Studies
810 West Markham Street
Little Rock, AR 72201
(501) 324-0514

Years In Operation: 6; **Grade Levels:** K-12; **Students Participating:** 26,000; **Community Participation:** community involvement in curriculum planning, use of community resources, use of human resources in the community, interaction with community organizations, community biracial committee, magnet review committee; **Social Goal:** multicultural education; **School Goal:** multicultural/social reconstructionist; **Primary Target:** minority students; **Curricular Aims:** multicultural education; **Instructional Aims:** multicultural/social reconstructionist; **Classroom Environment:** multicultural education; **School Practices:** ESL, culturally diverse faculty, parental involvement in school policy decisions, human relations training for teachers, community involvement in school policy decisions, inservice teacher training in multicultural education, interracial student council, ethnic studies curriculum; **Group Studied:** African Americans; **Elements Studied:** art, attitudes, beliefs, culture and personality, history, kinship structure, language, literature, material culture, music, religion, social customs, social organization, social structure, values; **Participating Disciplines:** social studies, international studies; **Locally Produced Materials:** yes.

PULASKI COUNTY SPECIAL
Brenda Spriggs Bowles
Coordinator of Multicultural Curriculum Development
925 East Dixon Road, P.O. Box 8601
Little Rock, AR 72216
(501) 490-2000

Years In Operation: 8; **Grade Levels:** K-12; **Students Participating:** 21,694; **Community Participation:** community involvement in curriculum planning, use of community resources, use of human resources in the community, interaction with community organizations; **Social Goal:** multicultural education; **School Goal:** multicultural education; **Primary Target:** all students; **Curricular Aims:** multicultural/social reconstructionist; **Instructional Aims:** multicultural/social reconstructionist; **Classroom Environment:** multicultural/social reconstructionist; **School Practices:** culturally diverse faculty, parental involvement in school policy decisions, culturally diverse staff, human relations training for teachers, inservice teacher training in multicultural education, student involvement in school policy decisions, human relations training for students, bicultural curriculum, standard English as a second dialect; **Elements Studied:** art, attitudes, beliefs, body language, culture and personality, dialect, foods, history, language, literature, material culture, music, physical characteristics, religion, social customs, social organization, social structure, values; **Locally Produced Materials:** yes.

CALIFORNIA

ANAHEIM UNION HIGH
Janice Billings, Ph.D.
501 Crescent Way
Anaheim, CA 92801
(714) 999-3568

Years In Operation: 3; **Grade Levels:** 7-12; **Community Participation:** use of community resources, use of human resources in the community, study of the community, interaction with community organizations; **Social Goal:** multicultural education; **School Goal:** multicultural education; **Primary Target:** all students; **Curricular Aims:** multicultural/social reconstructionist; **Instructional Aims:** multicultural/social reconstructionist; **Classroom Environment:** multicultural education; **School Practices:** transitional bilingual education, culturally diverse faculty, community involvement in school policy decisions, inservice teacher training in multicultural education, human relations training for students, bicultural curriculum, ethnic studies curriculum; **Groups Studied:** African Americans, Arab Americans, Asian/Pacific Islander Americans, Hispanic (Latino/Chicano) Americans, Native Americans; **Elements Studied:** art, beliefs, culture and personality, foods, history, literature, music, religion, social customs; **Participating Disciplines:** English, humanities, language arts, music, social studies.

ANTELOPE VALLEY UNION HIGH
Carmen Walker
44811 North Sierra Hwy.
Lancaster, CA 93534
(805) 538-0304

Years In Operation: 4; **Grade Levels:** 9-12; **Students Participating:** 6,000; **Community Participation:** use of resources in the community, interaction with community organizations; **Social Goal:** human relations; **School Goal:** human relations; **Primary Target:** all students; **Curricular Aims:** human relations; **Instructional Aims:** human relations; **Classroom Environment:** single-group studies; **School Practices:** ESL, culturally diverse faculty, Spanish as a second language; **Elements Studied:** beliefs, culture and personality, history.

BAKERSFIELD CITY
Henri Sakamaki
Assistant Superintendent of Instruction
1300 Baker Street
Bakersfield, CA 93305
(805) 631-5840

Years In Operation: 7; **Grade Levels:** K-8; **Students Participating:** 26,000; **Community Participation:** use of community resources, use of human resources in the community, interaction with community organizations; **Social Goal:** multicultural education; **School Goal:** human relations; **Primary Target:** all students; **Curricular Aims:** multicultural/social reconstructionist; **Instructional Aims:** multicultural education; **Classroom Environment:** multicultural education; **School Practices:** transitional bilingual education, ESL, culturally diverse faculty, human relations training for teachers, community involvement in school policy decisions, inservice teacher training in multicultural education, Spanish as a second language, student involvement in school policy decisions, human relations training for students, bilingual curriculum, bicultural curriculum; **Locally Produced Materials:** yes.

Baldwin Park
Anna M. Perez
Coordinator, Bilingual Education & Cultural Diversity
3699 North Holly Avenue
Baldwin Park, CA 91706
(818) 962-3311 ext. 4317

Bellflower Unified
Dr. Linda Gresik
Principal of English Language Development Programs
Las Flores Elementary
10039 East Palm
Bellflower, CA 90706
(310) 804-6565

Years In Operation: 5; **Grade Levels:** K-6; **Students Participating:** 343; **Community Participation:** interaction with community organizations; **Social Goal:** multicultural education; **School Goal:** multicultural education; **Primary Target:** low achieving students; **Curricular Aims:** multicultural education; **Instructional Aims:** multicultural education; **Classroom Environment:** multicultural/social reconstructionist; **School Practices:** transitional bilingual education, ESL, culturally diverse faculty, parental involvement in school policy decisions, Spanish as a second language, multilingual curriculum, standard English as a second dialect; **Locally Produced Materials:** yes.

Burbank Unified
Andrea Candy
330 North Buena Vista
Burbank, CA 91505
(818) 558-5345

Students Participating: 12,867; **Social Goal:** human relations; **School Goal:** human relations; **Primary Target:** all students; **Curricular Aims:** teaching the culturally different; **Instructional Aims:** multicultural/social reconstructionist; **Classroom Environment:** human relations; **School Practices:** transitional bilingual education, ESL, culturally diverse faculty, parental involvement in school policy decisions, culturally diverse staff, human relations training for teachers, community involvement in school policy decisions, strong school-community public relations effort, inservice teacher training in multicultural education, Spanish as a second language, student involvement in school policy decisions, bilingual curriculum, multilingual curriculum.

Capistrano Unified
Jody Wiencek
Title VII Coordinator
1101 Calle Puente
San Clemente, CA 92972
(714) 492-3456

Years In Operation: 2; **Grade Levels:** K-1; **Students Participating:** 120; **Community Participation:** community involvement in curriculum planning, use of community resources, use of human resources in the community, community based instructional program, interaction with community organizations, parent advisory committee; **Social Goal:** multicultural education; **School Goal:** multicultural/social reconstructionist; **Primary Target:** all students; **Curricular Aims:** multicultural/social reconstructionist; **Instructional Aims:** multicultural/social reconstructionist; **Classroom Environment:** multicultural/social reconstructionist; **School Practices:** transitional bilingual education, ESL, remedial classes, culturally diverse faculty, parental involvement in school policy decisions, culturally diverse staff, community involvement in school policy decisions, strong school-community public relations effort, Spanish as a second language, interracial student council, bilingual curriculum, bicultural curriculum, standard English as a second dialect, ethnic studies curriculum; **Groups Studied:** African Americans, Hispanic (Latino/Chicano) Americans, Native Americans; **Elements Studied:** art, attitudes, beliefs, culture and personality, foods, language, literature, material culture, music, social customs, social organization, social structure; **Participating Disciplines:** art, language arts, mathematics, reading, social studies.

Chino
George Gonzalez
Director of Bilingual Education
5130 Riverside Drive
Chino, CA 91710
(909) 628-1201 ext. 1330

Clovis Unified
Dr. Thomas E. Russell
Coordinator, Community Relations
1450 Herndon Avenue
Clovis, CA 93611
(209) 297-4000 ext. 2290

Years In Operation: 8; **Grade Levels:** K-12; **Students Participating:** 26,042; **Community Participation:** community involvement in curriculum planning, interaction with community organizations; **Social Goal:** multicultural education; **School Goal:** multicultural education; **Primary Target:** all students; **Curricular Aims:** multicultural/social reconstructionist; **Instructional Aims:** single-group studies; **Classroom Environment:** multicultural/social reconstructionist; **School Practices:** transitional bilingual education, ESL, culturally diverse faculty, parental involvement in school policy decisions, culturally diverse staff, community involvement in school policy decisions, strong school-community public relations effort, inservice teacher training in multicultural education, student involvement in curriculum planning, Spanish as a second language, student involvement in school policy decisions, interracial student council, human relations training for students, professionally staffed community relations office, bilingual curriculum, student human relations council, multilingual curriculum, ethnic studies curriculum; **Groups Studied:** African Americans, Asian/Pacific Islander Americans, Hispanic (Latino/Chicano) Americans, Native Americans; **Elements Studied:** art, attitudes, beliefs, culture and personality, dialect, foods, history, literature, music, religion, social customs; **Participating Disciplines:** art, English, health, mathematics, music, reading, science.

CONEJO VALLEY UNIFIED
Claudia Spellman
English Language Development
1400 East Hanes Road
Thousand Oaks, CA 91362
(805) 497-9511

Years In Operation: 20; **Grade Levels:** K-12; **Students Participating:** 17,763; **Community Participation:** community involvement in curriculum planning, use of community resources, use of human resources in the community, study of the community, interaction with community organizations; **Social Goal:** multicultural education; **School Goal:** human relations; **Primary Target:** all students; **Curricular Aims:** multicultural/social reconstructionist; **Instructional Aims:** multicultural/social reconstructionist; **Classroom Environment:** multicultural/social reconstructionist; **School Practices:** ESL, culturally diverse staff, human relations training for teachers, community involvement in school policy decisions, strong school-community public relations effort, inservice teacher training in multicultural education, student involvement in curriculum planning, Spanish as a second language, student involvement in school policy decisions, interracial student council, human relations training for students, Asian language(s), ethnic studies curriculum; **Groups Studied:** African Americans, Arab Americans, Asian/Pacific Islander Americans, French Americans, German Americans, Greek Americans, Hispanic (Latino/Chicano) Americans, Iranian Americans, Irish Americans, Italian Americans, Native Americans, Portuguese Americans, Scandinavian Americans, Slavic Americans; **Elements Studied:** art, attitudes, beliefs, body language, culture and personality, dialect, drama, foods, history, kinship structure, language, literature, material culture, music, physical characteristics, religion, social customs, social organization, social structure, values; **Participating Disciplines:** art, business, English, foreign languages, health, home economics, humanities, industrial arts, language arts, mathematics, music, physical education, reading, science, social studies, theater; **Locally Produced Materials:** yes.

EAST SIDE UNION HIGH
Lois Freeman
Assistant Director of Instruction
830 North Capital Avenue
San Jose, CA 95133
(408) 272-6474

Grade Levels: 9-12; **Community Participation:** use of community resources; **Social Goal:** multicultural education; **School Goal:** multicultural/social reconstructionist; **Primary Target:** all students; **Curricular Aims:** multicultural education; **Instructional Aims:** multicultural education; **Classroom Environment:** multicultural education; **School Practices:** transitional bilingual education, ESL, remedial classes, culturally diverse faculty, parental involvement in school policy decisions, community involvement in school policy decisions, strong school-community public relations effort, inservice teacher training in multicultural education, Spanish as a second language, interracial student council, bilingual curriculum, Asian language(s); **Locally Produced Materials:** yes; **Materials Available for Purchase:** yes.

FOLSOM-CORDOVA UNIFIED
Judy Lewis
2460 Cordova Lane
Rancho Cordova, CA 95670
(916) 635-6815

Years In Operation: 15; **Grade Levels:** K-12; **Students Participating:** 13,242; **Community Participation:** community involvement in curriculum planning, use of community resources, interaction with community organizations, resource center with focus on Southeast Asia, staff newsletter; **Social Goal:** human relations; **School Goal:** teaching the culturally different; **Primary Target:** all students; **Curricular Aims:** multicultural education; **Instructional Aims:** teaching the culturally different; **Classroom Environment:** multicultural education; **School Practices:** ESL, remedial classes, culturally diverse faculty, parental involvement in school policy decisions, community involvement in school policy decisions, strong school-community public relations effort, inservice teacher training in multicultural education; **Elements Studied:** art, attitudes, beliefs, foods, history, kinship structure, language, literature, material culture, music, physical characteristics, religion, social customs, social organization, values; **Locally Produced Materials:** yes; **Materials Available for Purchase:**

THE SOUTHEST ASIA COMMUNITY RESOURCE CENTER

#9512 *Handbook for Teaching Armenian Speaking Students*, Avakian, Ghazarian, 1995, 90 pages, $7.00. No carton discount.

#9411 *Parent Involvement in School: A Handbook for Language Minority Parents and School Personnel (Vietnamese Glossary & Summary)*, Huynh Dinh Te, 1994, $5.00. No carton discount.

#9410 *Amerasians from Vietnam: A California Study*, Chung & Le, 1994, $7.00. No carton discount.

#9409 *Proceedings on the Conference on Champa*, 1994, $7.00. No carton discount.

#9308 *Selected Resources: People from Cambodia, Laos, & Vietnam*, Lewis, ed., $5.00. No carton discount.

#9207 *Minority Cultures of Laos: Kammu, Lua', Lahu, Hmong, and Mien*, Lewis, Kam Raw, Vang, Elliott, Matisoff, Yang, Crystal, Saephran, 1992, 402 pages, $15.00. Carton discount $12.00, 16 per carton.

#S8801 *Handbook for Teaching Hmong-Speaking Students*, Bliatout, Downing, Lewis, Yang, 1988, $4.50. Carton discount for lots of 58, $3.50.

#S8802 *Handbook for Teaching Khmer-Speaking Students*, Ouk, Huffman, Lewis, 1988, $5.50. Carton discount for lots of 40, $4.50.

#S8903 *Handbook for Teaching Lao-Speaking Students*, Luangpraseut, Lewis, 1988, $5.50. Carton discount for lots of 42, $4.50.

#S8904 *Introduction to the Indochinese and their Cultures*, Chhim, Luangpraseut, Te, 1989, 1994, $9.00. Carton discount, $7.00.

#S8805 *English-Hmong Bilingual Dictionary of School Terminology: Cov Lus Mis Kuj Txhais ua Lus Hmoob*, Huynh D Te, translated by Lue Vang, 1988, $2.00. No carton discount.

#S9006 *Vietnamese Language Materials Sourcebook*, Huynh Dinh Te, 1990, $2.00. No carton discount.

Make payable to Folsom Cordova USD/SEACRC. Add California tax if applicable. For orders under $30.00, add $2.00 shipping and handling per copy. For orders over $30.00, add 10% shipping and handling. If you wish UPS for quantity orders, please request it.

#S9999	*CONTEXT: Southeast Asians & other newcomers in California*	
	Annual subscription	$10.00
#R001	Lao Alphabet Poster	$3.50
#R002	Lao Primer	$4.00
#R003	Lao 1st Grade Reader	$5.00
#R004	Lao 2nd Grade Reader	$5.50
#R005	Lao 3rd Grade Reader	$6.50
#R006	Hmong Primer	$4.00
#R007	Hmong Dictionary, Xiong, (Hmoob Ntsuab)	$30.00
#R008	1992 Faire Poster	$3.00

Make payable to Folsom Cordova USD/SEACRC. Includes tax. $1.00 shipping/handling per item up to $30.00. Over $30.00, 10% s/h.

Grandmother's Path, Grandfather's Way, Vang & Lewis, 1984, 1990, $14.95 plus $2.00 shipping/handling, CA tax. Make payable to Lue Vang, PO Box 423, Rancho Cordova, CA, 95741-0423.

Fremont Unified
Dr. Beth Robinson
Assistant Superintendent Instruction
4210 Technology Drive
Fremont, CA 94538
(510) 659-2583

Years In Operation: 1; **Grade Levels:** K-12; **Students Participating:** 30,000; **Community Participation:** community involvement in curriculum planning, use of community resources, use of human resources in the community, a community based instructional program, study of the community, interaction with community organizations; **Social Goal:** multicultural education; **School Goal:** multicultural/social reconstructionist; **Primary Target:** all students; **Curricular Aims:** multicultural/social reconstructionist; **Instructional Aims:** multicultural/social reconstructionist; **Classroom Environment:** multicultural/social reconstructionist; **School Practices:** transitional bilingual education, ESL, remedial classes, culturally diverse faculty, parental involvement in school policy decisions, culturally diverse staff, human relations training for teachers, community involvement in school policy decisions, strong school-community public relations effort, inservice teacher training in multicultural education, student involvement in curriculum planning, Spanish as a second language, student involvement in school policy decisions, interracial student council, human relations training for students, bilingual curriculum, student human relations council, bicultural curriculum, multilingual curriculum, standard English as a second dialect, Asian language(s), ethnic studies curriculum; **Groups Studied:** African Americans, Asian/Pacific Islander Americans, Hispanic (Latino/Chicano) Americans, Iranian Americans, Native Americans; **Elements Studied:** art, attitudes, beliefs, body language, culture and personality, dialect, drama, foods, history, language, literature, music, physical characteristics, religion, social customs, social organization, social structure, values; **Participating Disciplines:** foreign languages, humanities, language arts, music, reading, social studies, theater; **Locally Produced Materials:** yes.

Fresno Unified
Dr. Florentino Noriega
Associate Superintendent
Tulare & M Streets
Fresno, CA 93721
(209) 265-2972

Years In Operation: 22; **Grade Levels:** K-12; **Students Participating:** 25,000; **Community Participation:** community involvement in curriculum planning, use of community resources, use of human resources in the community, a community based instructional program, interaction with community organizations; **Social Goal:** multicultural education; **School Goal:** human relations; **Primary Target:** all students; **Curricular Aims:** multicultural education; **Instructional Aims:** multicultural education; **Classroom Environment:** multicultural/social reconstructionist; **School Practices:** transitional bilingual education, ESL, culturally diverse faculty, parental involvement in school policy decisions, culturally diverse staff, community involvement in school policy decisions, strong school-community public relations effort, inservice teacher training in multicultural education, student involvement in curriculum planning, Spanish as a second language, student involvement in school policy decisions, interracial student council, professionally staffed community relations office, bilingual curriculum, professionally staffed human relations team, bicultural curriculum, multilingual curriculum, standard English as a second dialect, Asian language(s), ethnic studies curriculum; **Groups Studied:** African Americans, Asian/Pacific Islander Americans, Hispanic (Latino/Chicano) Americans; **Elements Studied:** art, attitudes, beliefs, foods, history, language, literature, music, social organization, social structure, values; **Participating Disciplines:** art, foreign languages, humanities, language arts, social studies; **Locally Produced Materials:** yes.

FULLERTON JOINT UNION HIGH
Kay Selway
District Programs Specialist
780 Beechwood Avenue
Fullerton, CA 92633
(714) 671-4369

GLENDALE UNIFIED
Judy Sanchez
223 North Jackson Street
Glendale, CA 91206
(818) 241-3111 ext. 457

Years In Operation: 21; **Grade Levels:** K-12; **Students Participating:** 29,000; **Community Participation:** community involvement in curriculum planning, use of community resources, use of human resources in the community, interaction with community organizations, advisory councils; **Social Goal:** human relations; **School Goal:** human relations; **Primary Target:** all students; **Curricular Aims:** multicultural education; **Instructional Aims:** multicultural/social reconstructionist; **Classroom Environment:** single-group studies; **School Practices:** transitional bilingual education, ESL, remedial classes, culturally diverse faculty, parental involvement in school policy decisions, culturally diverse staff, human relations training for teachers, community involvement in school policy decisions, strong school-community public relations effort, inservice teacher training in multicultural education, student involvement in school policy decisions, interracial student council, human relations training for students, bilingual curriculum, multilingual curriculum; **Locally Produced Materials:** yes; **Materials Available for Purchase:** ESL Curriculum for Elementary and Secondary Grades, Service Guide for Limited English Proficient Students.

Grant Joint Union High
Roberta Mayor
Assistant Superintendent of Instruction
1333 Grand Avenue
Sacramento, CA 95838
(916) 263-6228

Grade Levels: 7-12; **Students Participating:** 10,000; **Community Participation:** use of community resources, interaction with community organizations; **Social Goal:** multicultural education; **School Goal:** multicultural education; **Primary Target:** all students; **Curricular Aims:** multicultural education; **Instructional Aims:** multicultural education; **Classroom Environment:** multicultural/social reconstructionist; **School Practices:** transitional bilingual education, ESL, remedial classes, human relations training for teachers, community involvement in school policy decisions, strong school-community public relations effort, inservice teacher training in multicultural education, student involvement in school policy decisions, interracial student council, human relations training for students, standard English as a second dialect, ethnic studies curriculum; **Groups Studied:** African Americans, Asian/Pacific Islander Americans, Hispanic (Latino/Chicano) Americans; **Elements Studied:** culture and personality, history, literature, social customs; **Participating Disciplines:** foreign languages, humanities, social studies.

Grossmont Union High
Jean Kerr
Director of Special Programs
1100 Murray Drive
El Cajon, CA 92020
(619) 465-3131 ext. 370

Grade Levels: 9-12; **Students Participating:** 20,000; **Community Participation:** community involvement in curriculum planning, interaction with community organizations; **Social Goal:** multicultural education; **School Goal:** human relations; **Primary Target:** all students; **Curricular Aims:** multicultural education; **Instructional Aims:** multicultural education; **Classroom Environment:** single-group studies; **School Practices:** transitional bilingual education, ESL, remedial classes, human relations training for teachers, inservice teacher training in multicultural education, Spanish as a second language, human relations training for students, bilingual curriculum.

INGLEWOOD UNIFIED
Dr. Lowell Winston
Assistant Superintendent, Educational Services
401 S. Inglewood Avenue
Inglewood, CA 90301
(310) 419-2724

Years In Operation: 20; **Grade Levels:** K-12; **Students Participating:** 16,500; **Community Participation:** community involvement in curriculum planning, use of community resources, use of human resources in the community, interaction with community organizations, community participation in strategic planning; **Social Goal:** teaching the culturally different; **School Goal:** human relations; **Primary Target:** all students; **Curricular Aims:** multicultural education; **Instructional Aims:** multicultural/social reconstructionist; **Classroom Environment:** multicultural/social reconstructionist; **School Practices:** transitional bilingual education, ESL, culturally diverse staff, human relations training for teachers, community involvement in school policy decisions, strong school-community public relations effort, inservice teacher training in multicultural education, student involvement in curriculum planning, Spanish as a second language, student involvement in school policy decisions, interracial student council, human relations training for students, professionally staffed community relations office, bilingual curriculum, professionally staffed human relations team, bicultural curriculum, multilingual curriculum, standard English as a second dialect, ethnic studies curriculum; **Groups Studied:** African Americans, Asian/Pacific Islander Americans, Hispanic (Latino/Chicano) Americans; **Elements Studied:** attitudes, beliefs, body language, social organization; **Participating Disciplines:** art, business, foreign languages, humanities, language arts, mathematics, music, physical education, science, social studies; **Locally Produced Materials:** yes.

LA MESA-SPRING VALLEY
Kathy Cupp
Coordinator, Special Programs
4750 Date Avenue
La Mesa, CA 91941-5293
(619) 668-5700 ext. 421

LODI UNIFIED
Carol Rivas
Coordinator, Multilingual/Multicultural Programs
1305 East Vine Street
Lodi, CA 95240-3148
(209) 331-7026

Los Angeles County
Judith G. Moses
Consultant-Multicultural Education
CPIT Rm 299, 9300 Imperial Hwy.
Downey, CA 90242
(310) 922-6323

Years In Operation: 20; **Grade Levels:** K-12; **Students Participating:** 1,465,597; **Community Participation:** community involvement in curriculum planning, use of community resources, study of the community; **Social Goal:** multicultural education; **School Goal:** multicultural/social reconstructionist; **Primary Target:** all students; **Curricular Aims:** multicultural/social reconstructionist; **Instructional Aims:** multicultural/social reconstructionist; **Classroom Environment:** multicultural/social reconstructionist; **School Practices:** transitional bilingual education, ESL, remedial classes, culturally diverse faculty, parental involvement in school policy decisions, culturally diverse staff, human relations training for teachers, community involvement in school policy decisions, inservice teacher training in multicultural education, student involvement in curricular planning, Spanish as a second language, student involvement in school policy decisions, interracial student council, human relations training for students, bilingual curriculum, student human relations council, bicultural curriculum, multilingual curriculum, Asian language(s); **Locally Produced Materials:** yes.

Los Angeles Unified
Dr. Evangelina Stockwell
Assistant Superintendent, Intergroup Relations
450 North Grand Avenue, RM P-318
Los Angeles, CA 90012
(213) 625-6579

Years In Operation: 25; **Grade Levels:** K-12; **Students Participating:** 600,000; **Community Participation:** use of community resources, use of human resources in the community, District Chapter I Parents' Advisory Committee, District Bilingual Parent Advisory Committee, Parents Community/Service Branch: Parents Collaborative; **Social Goal:** multicultural education; **School Goal:** multicultural/social reconstructionist; **Primary Target:** all students; **Curricular Aims:** multicultural/social reconstructionist; **Instructional Aims:** multicultural/social reconstructionist; **Classroom Environment:** multicultural/social reconstructionist; **School Practices:** transitional bilingual education, ESL, culturally diverse faculty, parental involvement in school policy decisions, culturally diverse staff, human relations training for teachers, community involvement in school policy decisions, strong school-community public relations effort, inservice teacher training in multicultural education, Spanish as a second language, interracial student council, human relations training for students, professionally staffed community relations office, bilingual curriculum, professionally staffed public relations team, student human relations council, bicultural curriculum, multilingual curriculum, standard English as a second dialect, Asian language(s), ethnic studies curriculum; **Groups Studied:** African Americans, Asian/ Pacific Islander Americans, Hispanic (Latino/Chicano) Americans, Native Americans; **Elements Studied:** art, attitudes, beliefs, body language, culture and personality, history, language, literature, material culture, music, social customs, social organization, social structure, values, current issues of concern; **Participating Disciplines:** art, English, humanities, language arts, mathematics, music, reading, science, social studies; **Locally Produced Materials:** yes.

MODESTO CITY ELEMENTARY
Edmund Lee
Supervisor of Bilingual Education
426 Locust Street
Modesto, CA 95351
(209) 576-4057

Years In Operation: 10; **Grade Levels:** K-12; **Students Participating:** 29,000; **Community Participation:** use of human resources in the community; **Social Goal:** multicultural education; **School Goal:** human relations; **Primary Target:** all students; **Curricular Aims:** teaching the culturally different; **Instructional Aims:** multicultural education; **Classroom Environment:** single-group studies; **School Practices:** transitional bilingual education, ESL, culturally diverse faculty, culturally diverse staff, community involvement in school policy decisions, strong school-community public relations effort, inservice teacher training in multicultural education, Spanish as a second language, bilingual curriculum, multilingual curriculum; **Elements Studied:** foods, history, language, literature, music.

MODESTO CITY HIGH
Edmund Lee
426 Locust Street
Modesto, CA 95351
(209) 576-4057

Years In Operation: 5; **Grade Levels:** K-12; **Students Participating:** 29,000; **Community Participation:** use of community resources, use of human resources in the community; **Social Goal:** human relations; **School Goal:** human relations; **Primary Target:** all students; **Curricular Aims:** human relations; **Instructional Aims:** human relations; **Classroom Environment:** multicultural education; **School Practices:** transitional bilingual education, ESL, remedial classes, culturally diverse faculty, parental involvement in school policy decisions, culturally diverse staff, community involvement in school policy decisions, Spanish as a second language, bilingual curriculum, bicultural curriculum, multicultural curriculum, Asian language(s); **Elements Studied:** art, language, literature, social customs; **Locally Produced Materials:** yes.

Mt. Diablo Unified
Linda Rondeau
1936 Carlotta Drive
Concord, CA 94519
(510) 682-8000 ext. 4026

Years In Operation: 23; **Grade Levels:** K-12; **Students Participating:** 34,000; **Community Participation:** use of community resources, use of human resources in the community, study of the community, interaction with community organizations; **Social Goal:** multicultural education; **School Goal:** teaching the culturally different; **Primary Target:** all students; **Curricular Aims:** teaching the culturally different; **Instructional Aims:** multicultural education; **Classroom Environment:** multicultural education; **School Practices:** transitional bilingual education, ESL, remedial classes, culturally diverse faculty, parental involvement in school policy decisions, human relations training for teachers, community involvement in school policy decisions, strong school-community public relations effort, inservice teacher training in multicultural education, Spanish as a second language, student involvement in school policy decisions, interracial student council, bilingual curriculum, bicultural curriculum, standard English as a second dialect.

Napa Valley Unified
Deborah Wallace
Bilingual Resource Teacher
2700 Kilburn Avenue
Napa, CA 94558
(707) 253-3678

Years In Operation: 6; **Grade Levels:** K-6; **Students Participating:** 600; **Community Participation:** use of community resources, use of human resources in the community, a community based instructional program, study of the community, interaction with community organizations, Junior Achievement, Hispanic Network, Healthy Start Community Liaison, community project grants; **Social Goal:** single-group studies; **School Goal:** multicultural education; **Primary Target:** all students; **Curricular Aims:** multicultural education; **Instructional Aims:** multicultural education; **Classroom Environment:** multicultural/social reconstructionist; **School Practices:** transitional bilingual education, ESL, remedial classes, culturally diverse faculty, parental involvement in school policy decisions, culturally diverse staff, human relations training for teachers, community involvement in school policy decisions, strong school-community public relations effort, inservice teacher training in multicultural education, student involvement in curriculum planning, Spanish as a second language, student involvement in school policy decisions, interracial student council, human relations training for students, professionally staffed community relations office, bilingual curriculum, bicultural curriculum, multilingual curriculum; **Elements Studied:** art, attitudes, body language, culture and personality, dialect, drama, foods, history, kinship structure, language, literature, music, religion, social customs, values; **Locally Produced Materials:** yes; **Materials Available for Purchase:** yes.

NORWALK-LA MIRADA UNIFIED
Lorelei Coddington
12820 Pioneer Blvd.
Norwalk, CA 90650-2894
(310) 868-0431 ext. 2149

Years In Operation: 3; **Grade Levels:** 2-7; **Students Participating:** 1,500; **Community Participation:** community involvement in curriculum planning, use of community resources, use of human resources in the community, study of the community, interaction with community organizations, partnerships with businesses; **Social Goal:** multicultural education; **School Goal:** multicultural education; **Primary Target:** all students; **Curricular Aims:** teaching the culturally different; **Instructional Aims:** multicultural/social reconstructionist; **Classroom Environment:** multicultural/social reconstructionist; **School Practices:** transitional bilingual education, ESL, remedial classes, parental involvement in school policy decisions, culturally diverse staff, human relations training for teachers, community involvement in school policy decisions, strong school-community public relations effort, inservice teacher training in multicultural education, student involvement in curricular planning, interracial student council, professionally staffed community relations office, bilingual curriculum, multilingual curriculum, ethnic studies curriculum; **Groups Studied:** African Americans, Arab Americans, Asian/Pacific Islander Americans, French Americans, German Americans, Greek Americans, Hispanic (Latino/Chicano) Americans, Iranian Americans, Irish Americans, Italian Americans, Native Americans, Portuguese Americans, Scandinavian Americans, Slavic Americans; **Elements Studied:** art, attitudes, beliefs, body language, culture and personality, dialect, drama, foods, history, kinship structure, language, literature, material culture, music, physical characteristics, religion, social customs, social organization, social structure, values; **Participating Disciplines:** art, business, English, foreign languages, health, home economics, humanities, industrial arts, language arts, mathematics, music, physical education, reading, science, social studies, theater; **Locally Produced Materials:** yes.

OAKLAND UNIFIED
Irma Butzen
Teacher on Special Assignment
202 Harper Bldg., 314 East 10th Street
Oakland, CA 94606
(510) 836-9244

Oceanside City Unified
James Shirley
District Program Specialist
2080 Mission Ave.
Oceanside, CA 92054
(619) 967-1322

Years In Operation: 15; **Grade Levels:** K-12; **Students Participating:** 19,000; **Community Participation:** use of community resources, use of human resources in the community, study of the community; **Social Goal:** multicultural education; **School Goal:** teaching the culturally different; **Primary Target:** all students; **Curricular Aims:** multicultural/social reconstructionist; **Instructional Aims:** human relations; **Classroom Environment:** multicultural/social reconstructionist; **School Practices:** transitional bilingual education, ESL, culturally diverse faculty, parental involvement in school policy decisions, interracial student council, bilingual curriculum, bicultural curriculum, multilingual curriculum; **Elements Studied:** art, beliefs, culture and personality, drama, foods, history, literature; **Participating Disciplines:** art, foreign languages, language arts, reading, social studies.

Oxnard Union High
Dr. Gary Davis
Assistant Superintendent/Educational Services
309 South K Street
Oxnard, CA 93030
(805) 385-2521

Years In Operation: 4; **Grade Levels:** 9-12; **Students Participating:** 12,000; **Community Participation:** community involvement in curriculum planning, use of community resources, use of human resources in the community, interaction with community organizations; **Social Goal:** multicultural education; **School Goal:** multicultural education; **Primary Target:** all students; **Curricular Aims:** multicultural education; **Instructional Aims:** human relations; **Classroom Environment:** multicultural/social reconstructionist; **School Practices:** transitional bilingual education, ESL, remedial classes, culturally diverse faculty, parental involvement in school policy decisions, culturally diverse staff, human relations training for teachers, community involvement in school policy decisions, strong school-community public relations effort, inservice teacher training in multicultural education, student involvement in curriculum planning, Spanish as a second language, student involvement in school policy decisions, interracial student council, human relations training for students, professionally staffed community relations office, bilingual curriculum, professionally staffed community relations team, student human relations council, bicultural curriculum, multilingual curriculum, standard English as a second dialect, ethnic studies curriculum; **Groups Studied:** African Americans, Asian/Pacific Islander Americans, Hispanic (Latino/Chicano) Americans, Native Americans; **Elements Studied:** art, attitudes, beliefs, body language, culture and personality, dialect, drama, foods, history, kinship structure, language, literature, material culture, music, physical characteristics, religion, social customs, social organization, social structure, values; **Participating Disciplines:** art, business, English, foreign languages, health, home economics, humanities, industrial arts, language arts, mathematics, music, physical education, reading, science, social studies, theater.

SADDLEBACK VALLEY UNIFIED
Gloria Roelen
Coordinator, Bilingual/ESL Department
25631 Diseno Drive
Mission Viejo, CA 92691
(714) 580-3347

Years In Operation: 5; **Grade Levels:** K-12; **Students Participating:** 27,000; **Community Participation:** use of community resources, interaction with community organizations; **Social Goal:** teaching the culturally different; **School Goal:** teaching the culturally different; **Primary Target:** all students; **Curricular Aims:** teaching the culturally different; **Instructional Aims:** teaching the culturally different; **Classroom Environment:** single-group studies; **School Practices:** transitional bilingual education, ESL, human relations training for teachers, community involvement in school policy decisions, strong school-community public relations effort, inservice teacher training in multicultural education, student involvement in school policy decisions; **Elements Studied:** art, foods, history, language, material culture, music, social customs; **Participating Disciplines:** foreign languages, humanities, language arts, music, social studies.

SAN DIEGO CITY UNIFIED
Dr. Francine F. Williams
Instructional Team Leader/Director, Race & Human Relations
(619) 225-3580
Karen Toyohara
Resource Teacher, Race & Human Relations
(619) 225-3577
1775 Chatsworth Boulevard
San Diego, CA 92107-3709

Grade Levels: K-12; **Students Participating:** 40,000; **Community Participation:** community involvement in curriculum planning, use of community resources, use of human resources in the community, study of the community, interaction with community organizations; **Social Goal:** single-group studies; **School Goal:** multicultural education; **Primary Target:** all students; **Curricular Aims:** multicultural/social reconstructionist; **Instructional Aims:** multicultural/social reconstructionist; **School Practices:** human relations training for teachers, strong school-community public relations effort, inservice teacher training in multicultural education, human relations training for students, professionally staffed human relations team, bicultural curriculum, ethnic studies curriculum; **Groups Studied:** African Americans, Arab Americans, Asian/Pacific Islander Americans, French Americans, German Americans, Greek Americans, Hispanic (Latino/Chicano) Americans, Iranian Americans, Irish Americans, Italian Americans, Native Americans, Portuguese Americans, Scandinavian Americans, Slavic Americans; **Elements Studied:** art, attitudes, beliefs, culture and personality, drama, history, language, literature, music, social customs, values; **Participating Disciplines:** art, English, foreign languages, humanities, language arts, music, reading, science, social studies; **Locally Produced Materials:** yes; **Materials Available for Purchase:** yes.

San Francisco Unified
Roger Tom
Curriculum Director
2550 25th Avenue
San Francisco, CA 94116
(415) 759-2950
Legayer Avenida
Bilingual Educational Director
300 Seneca Avenue
San Francisco, CA 94112
(415) 469-4777

Years In Operation: 5; **Grade Levels:** K-12; **Students Participating:** 62,500; **Community Participation:** community involvement in curriculum planning, use of community resources, study of the community, interaction with community organizations; **Social Goal:** multicultural education, **School Goal:** multicultural education; **Primary Target:** all students; **Curricular Aims:** multicultural education; **Instructional Aims:** multicultural education; **Classroom Environment:** multicultural/social reconstructionist; **School Practices:** transitional bilingual education, ESL, remedial classes, culturally diverse faculty, parental involvement in school policy decisions, culturally diverse staff, inservice teacher training in multicultural education, Spanish as a second language, student involvement in school policy decisions, interracial student council, human relations training for students, bilingual curriculum, student human relations council, bicultural curriculum, multilingual curriculum, standard English as a second dialect, Asian language(s), ethnic studies curriculum; **Groups Studied:** African Americans, Asian/Pacific Islander Americans, Hispanic (Latino/Chicano) Americans; **Elements Studied:** art, attitudes, beliefs, culture and personality, foods, history, language, literature, material culture, music, values; **Participating Disciplines:** English, foreign languages, health, humanities, language arts, mathematics, reading, social studies; **Locally Produced Materials:** yes.

SAN JUAN UNIFIED

Isabel Johnson
Program Specialist
3738 Walnut Avenue
Carmichael, CA 95608
(916) 971-5260

Years In Operation: 19; **Grade Levels:** K-12; **Community Participation:** community involvement in curriculum planning, use of community resources, use of human resources in the community, interaction with community organizations; **Social Goal:** human relations; **School Goal:** human relations; **Primary Target:** all students; **Curricular Aims:** multicultural education; **Instructional Aims:** multicultural education; **Classroom Environment:** multicultural education; **School Practices:** ESL, parental involvement in school policy decisions, human relations training for teachers, community involvement in school policy decisions, inservice teacher training in multicultural education, bilingual curriculum, bicultural curriculum, multilingual curriculum, Native American language(s), ethnic studies curriculum; **Group Studied:** Native Americans; **Elements Studied:** art, attitudes, beliefs, culture and personality, foods, history, kinship structure, language, music, religion, social customs; **Participating Discipline:** Native American education; **Locally Produced Materials:** yes; **Materials Available for Purchase:** yes.

SANTA ANA UNIFIED

Vergil L. Hettick, Ph.D.
Director, Research and Evaluation
1405 French Street
Santa Ana, CA 92701
(714) 558-5850

Years In Operation: 20; **Grade Levels:** K-12; **Students Participating:** 48,000; **Community Participation:** use of community resources, use of human resources in the community, interaction with community organizations; **Social Goal:** single-group studies; **School Goal:** human relations; **Primary Target:** all students; **Curricular Aims:** multicultural education; **Instructional Aims:** multicultural education; **Classroom Environment:** multicultural education; **School Practices:** transitional bilingual education, ESL, culturally diverse faculty, parental involvement in school policy decisions, culturally diverse staff, community involvement in school policy decisions, strong school-community public relations effort, inservice teacher training in multicultural education, human relations training for students, professionally staffed community relations office, bilingual curriculum, bicultural curriculum, Asian language(s); **Elements Studied:** art, drama, foods, history, language, literature, music, social customs.

Simi Valley Unified
Becky Wetzel
875 East Cochran Street
Simi Valley, CA 93065
(805) 520-6560

Years In Operation: 4; **Grade Levels:** K-12; **Students Participating:** 18,000; **Community Participation:** community involvement in curriculum planning, use of community resources, interaction with community organizations; **Social Goal:** human relations; **School Goal:** human relations; **Primary Target:** all students; **Curricular Aims:** multicultural education; **Instructional Aims:** multicultural education; **Classroom Environment:** teaching the culturally different; **School Practices:** transitional bilingual education, ESL, culturally diverse faculty, parental involvement in school policy decisions, inservice teacher training in multicultural education, student involvement in curricular planning, Spanish as a second language, student involvement in school policy decisions, human relations training for students.

Ventura Unified
Floyd Beller
Indian Education Coordinator
120 East Santa Clara Street
Ventura, CA 93001
(805) 652-7273

Years In Operation: 22; **Grade Levels:** K-12; **Students Participating:** 950; **Community Participation:** use of community resources, use of human resources in the community, interaction with community organizations; **Social Goal:** multicultural/social reconstructionist; **School Goal:** human relations; **Primary Target:** low achieving students; **Curricular Aims:** single-group studies; **Instructional Aims:** teaching the culturally different; **Classroom Environment:** multicultural/social reconstructionist; **School Practices:** culturally diverse faculty, human relations training for teachers, inservice teacher training in multicultural education, student involvement in curricular planning, ethnic studies curriculum; **Group Studied:** Native Americans; **Elements Studied:** art, culture and personality, foods, history, kinship structure, literature, material culture, music, social structure, values; **Participating Disciplines:** art, English, language arts, mathematics, reading, science, social studies; **Locally Produced Materials:** yes.

COLORADO

ADAMS-ARAPAHOE
Helen Alexis
Coordinator of Multicultural Education
15751 East First Avenue
Aurora, CO 80011
(303) 340-0854

Years In Operation: 5; **Grade Levels:** K-12; **Students Participating:** 27,307; **Community Participation:** community involvement in curriculum planning, use of community resources, use of human resources in the community, community based instructional program, study of the community, interaction with community organizations; **Social Goal:** multicultural education; **School Goal:** multicultural/social reconstructionist; **Primary Target:** all students; **Curricular Aims:** multicultural/social reconstructionist; **Instructional Aims:** multicultural/social reconstructionist; **Classroom Environment:** multicultural/social reconstructionist; **School Practices:** ESL, culturally diverse faculty, human relations training for teachers, community involvement in school policy decisions, strong school-community public relations effort, inservice teacher training in multicultural education, interracial student council, professionally staffed community relations office, professionally staffed human relations team, Asian language(s), ethnic studies curriculum; **Groups Studied:** African Americans, French Americans, German Americans, Hispanic (Latino/Chicano) Americans, Native Americans; **Elements Studied:** art, attitudes, beliefs, drama, foods, literature, music, religion; **Participating Disciplines:** social studies; **Locally Produced Materials:** yes; **Materials Available for Purchase:** Multicultural Notebook ($70), Multicultural Calendar.

BOULDER VALLEY
Ray Sanchez
Multicultural Curriculum Specialist
P.O. Box 9011
Boulder, CO 80301
(303) 447-1010 ext. 6036

Cherry Creek
Carolyn Jones
Multicultural Coordinator
4700 South Yosemite Street
Englewood, CO 80111
(303) 773-1184; FAX: (303) 773-9370

Years In Operation: 6; **Grade Levels:** K-12; **Students Participating:** 22,373; **Community Participation:** community involvement in curriculum planning, use of community resources, use of human resources in the community, interaction with community organizations; **Social Goal:** multicultural/social reconstructionist; **School Goal:** multicultural/social reconstructionist; **Primary Target:** all students; **Curricular Aims:** multicultural/social reconstructionist; **Instructional Aims:** multicultural/social reconstructionist; **Classroom Environment:** multicultural/social reconstructionist; **School Practices:** transitional bilingual education, ESL, culturally diverse faculty, parental involvement in school policy decisions, human relations training for teachers, community involvement in school policy decisions, strong school-community public relations effort, inservice teacher training in multicultural education, student involvement in school policy decisions, interracial student council, human relations training for students, student human relations council; **Locally Produced Materials:** yes; **Materials Available for Purchase:** *Through the Eyes of the World* (Multicultural Bibliography).

Denver County
Josephine Thomas
900 Grant Street, 6th Floor
Denver, CO 80203
(303) 764-3491

Years In Operation: 1; **Grade Levels:** K-12; **Students Participating:** 62,000; **Community Participation:** use of human resources in the community, interaction with community organizations, Bilingual Parent Advisory Committee; **Social Goal:** human relations; **School Goal:** multicultural education; **Primary Target:** all students; **Curricular Aims:** multicultural education; **Instructional Aims:** multicultural education; **Classroom Environment:** single-group studies; **School Practices:** transitional bilingual education, ESL, culturally diverse faculty, parental involvement in school policy decisions, human relations training for teachers, community involvement in school policy decisions, inservice teacher training in multicultural education, Spanish as a second language, bilingual curriculum, standard English as a second dialect, ethnic studies curriculum; **Groups Studied:** African Americans, Asian/Pacific Islander Americans, Hispanic (Latino/Chicano) Americans, Native Americans, Russian Americans; **Elements Studied:** art, beliefs, culture and personality, foods, history, language, literature, music, social customs; **Participating Disciplines:** English, foreign languages, language arts, music, reading, social studies; **Locally Produced Materials:** yes.

DOUGLAS COUNTY
Dr. Ron Cabrera
Principal-Multicultural Administrative Liaison
400 North Heritage Road
Castle Rock, CO 80104
(303) 688-1731

Years In Operation: 3; **Grade Levels:** K-12; **Community Participation:** use of community resources, use of human resources in the community, study of the community, interaction with community organizations; **Social Goal:** single-group studies; **School Goal:** multicultural education; **Primary Target:** all students; **Curricular Aims:** multicultural/social reconstructionist; **Instructional Aims:** multicultural education; **Classroom Environment:** multicultural education; **School Practices:** remedial classes, culturally diverse staff, community involvement in school policy decisions, interracial student council, professionally staffed community relations office; **Locally Produced Materials:** yes.

JEFFERSON COUNTY
Irene Griego
Program Coordinator
80 South Teller Street
Lakewood, CO 80226
(303) 238-1257

MESA COUNTY VALLEY
Dolores Pitman
Coordinator, Equity and Dropout Prevention
2115 Grand Avenue
Grand Junction, CO 81501
(303) 245-2422; FAX: (303) 245-2714

Years In Operation: 6; **Grade Levels:** K-12; **Students Participating:** 17,888; **Community Participation:** use of human resources in the community, interaction with community organizations; **Social Goal:** single-group studies; **School Goal:** multicultural education; **Primary Target:** all students; **Curricular Aims:** multicultural education; **Instructional Aims:** multicultural/social reconstructionist; **Classroom Environment:** multicultural/social reconstructionist; **School Practices:** ESL, remedial classes, culturally diverse faculty, parental involvement in school policy decisions, culturally diverse staff, human relations training for teachers, community involvement in school policy decisions, strong school-community public relations effort, inservice teacher training in multicultural education, student involvement in curriculum planning, Spanish as a second language, student involvement in school policy decisions, standard English as a second dialect, ethnic studies curriculum; **Groups Studied:** African Americans, Asian/Pacific Islander Americans, Hispanic (Latino/Chicano) Americans, Native Americans; **Elements Studied:** art, attitudes, beliefs, body language, culture and personality, foods, history, language, literature, music, physical characteristics, religion, social customs, values; **Participating Disciplines:** foreign languages, humanities, language arts, social studies.

Poudre

Barbara Spaulding
Project Manager, Multicultural Education Diversity
2407 La Porte Avenue
Fort Collins, CO 80521
(970) 482-7420

Years In Operation: 1; **Community Participation:** use of community resources, use of human resources in the community, study of the community, interaction with community organizations; **Social Goal:** multicultural education; **School Goal:** multicultural education; **Primary Target:** minority students; **Curricular Aims:** multicultural/social reconstructionist; **Instructional Aims:** multicultural education; **Classroom Environment:** multicultural/social reconstructionist; **School Practices:** ESL, remedial classes, parental involvement in school policy decisions, culturally diverse staff, community involvement in school policy decisions, strong school-community public relations effort, inservice teacher training in multicultural education, Spanish as a second language, student involvement in school policy decisions, human relations training for students, bilingual curriculum, bicultural curriculum, ethnic studies curriculum; **Groups Studied:** African Americans, Asian/Pacific Islander Americans, Greek Americans, Hispanic (Latino/Chicano) Americans, Native Americans; **Participating Disciplines:** English, humanities, language arts; **Locally Produced Materials:** yes.

Thompson

Dr. Nancy Wear
Director, Career Education
535 North Douglas Avenue
Loveland, CO 80537
(970) 669-3940 ext. 359

Years In Operation: 1; **Grade Levels:** K-12; **Students Participating:** 13,1000; **Community Participation:** community involvement in curriculum planning, use of community resources, use of human resources in the community, community based instructional program, study of the community, interaction with community organizations; **Social Goal:** single-group studies; **School Goal:** multicultural education; **Primary Target:** all students; **Curricular Aims:** multicultural/social reconstructionist; **Instructional Aims:** multicultural/social reconstructionist; **Classroom Environment:** multicultural/social reconstructionist; **School Practices:** ESL, culturally diverse faculty, parental involvement in school policy decisions, culturally diverse staff, community involvement in school policy decisions, strong school-community public relations effort, inservice teacher training in multicultural education, student involvement in curriculum planning, student involvement in school policy decisions, interracial student council.

CONNECTICUT

HARTFORD
Adrienne Snair Trother
300 Wethersfield Avenue
Hartford, CT 06114
(203) 722-8665

Years In Operation: 21; **Grade Levels:** K-12; **Students Participating:** 25,377; **Community Participation:** community involvement in curriculum planning, use of community resources, use of human resources in the community, multicultural awareness programs; **Social Goal:** multicultural/social reconstructionist; **School Goal:** teaching the culturally different; **Primary Target:** all students; **Curricular Aims:** multicultural education; **Instructional Aims:** multicultural/social reconstructionist; **Classroom Environment:** multicultural/social reconstructionist; **School Practices:** transitional bilingual education, ESL, remedial classes, culturally diverse faculty, parental involvement in school policy decisions, culturally diverse staff, human relations training for teachers, inservice teacher training in multicultural education, bilingual curriculum, standard English as a second dialect, ethnic studies curriculum; **Groups Studied:** African Americans, Asian/Pacific Islander Americans, French Americans, German Americans, Greek Americans, Hispanic (Latino/Chicano) Americans, Irish Americans, Italian Americans, Native Americans, Portuguese Americans, Scandinavian Americans, Slavic Americans; **Elements Studied:** art, attitudes, beliefs, body language, culture and personality, dialect, drama, foods, history, kinship structure, language, literature, material culture, music, physical characteristics, religion, social customs, social organization, social structure, values; **Participating Disciplines:** language arts, social studies.

NEW HAVEN
Charles E. Warner
Supervisor of Instruction
54 Meadow Street-Gateway
New Haven, CT 06519
(203) 946-8810 ext. 8888

Years In Operation: 1; **Grade Levels:** K-12; **Students Participating:** 18,000; **Community Participation:** community involvement in curriculum planning, use of community resources, use of human resources in the community, a community based instructional program, study of the community, interaction with community organiza-

tions; **Social Goal:** human relations; **School Goal:** multicultural/social reconstructionist; **Primary Target:** all students; **Curricular Aims:** multicultural/social reconstructionist; **Instructional Aims:** multicultural/social reconstructionist; **Classroom Environment:** multicultural/social reconstructionist; **School Practices:** transitional bilingual education, ESL, remedial classes, culturally diverse faculty, parental involvement in school policy decisions, culturally diverse staff, human relations training for teachers, community involvement in school policy decisions, strong school-community public relations effort, inservice teacher training in multicultural education, student involvement in curricular planning, Spanish as a second language, student involvement in school policy decisions, interracial student council, human relations training for students, bilingual curriculum; **Elements Studied:** attitudes, beliefs, material culture, social customs, social organization, social structure, values; **Participating Disciplines:** art, English, foreign languages, health, home economics, humanities, language arts, music, physical education, reading, science, social studies, theater.

Stamford
Dr. Bettye Fletcher
Coordinator for Diversity Education
P.O. Box 9310
Stamford, CT 06901
(203) 977-5105

Waterbury
Richard Cherubino
Principal
Jose Palermo
Supervisor, Bilingual Education
236 Grand Street
Waterbury, CT 06702
(203) 574-8162

DELAWARE

Brandywine
C. Lawler Rogers, Sr.
Supervisor of Fine Arts
1000 Pennsylvania Avenue
Claymont, DE 19703
(302) 792-3830

COLONIAL
Jerry Joyner
318 East Basin Road
New Castle, DE 19720
(302) 323-2727

Years In Operation: 4; **Grade Levels:** K-12; **Community Participation:** community involvement in curriculum planning, use of community resources, use of human resources in the community, study of the community, interaction with community organizations; **Social Goal:** multicultural education; **School Goal:** multicultural education; **Primary Target:** all students; **Curricular Aims:** multicultural education; **Instructional Aims:** multicultural education; **Classroom Environment:** multicultural/social reconstructionist; **School Practices:** parental involvement in school policy decisions, human relations training for teachers, community involvement in school policy decisions, strong school-community public relations effort, inservice teacher training in multicultural education, Spanish as a second language, human relations training for students, multilingual curriculum.

DISTRICT OF COLUMBIA

DISTRICT OF COLUMBIA
Thomasina M. Portis
Associate & Director, Multicultural/Values Education
Student Efficacy, Linkages, and Collaboration
Center for Systematic Educational Change
Weatherless Building
Burns & C Streets, SE
Washington, D.C. 20019
(202) 645-0197; FAX: (202) 645-0204

Mary Ellen Gallegos
Director, Minority Affairs Branch
Roosevelt Administrative Unit
13th and Upshur Streets, NW
Washington, D.C. 20011
(202) 576-8850; FAX: (202) 576-8861

FLORIDA

Alachua County
Christiana Shaw
620 East University Avenue
Gainesville, FL 32601
(904) 955-7300

Bay County
Joann Cox
1311 Balboa Avenue
Panama City, FL 32401
(904) 872-4332

Brevard County
Irene Ramnarine
Social Studies Resource Teacher
2700 St. Johns Street
Melborne, FL 30060
(407) 631-1911

Years In Operation: 3; **Grade Levels:** K-12; **Students Participating:** 65,000; **Community Participation:** community involvement in curriculum planning, use of community resources, use of human resources in the community, interaction with community organizations; **Social Goal:** human relations; **Primary Target:** all students; **Curricular Aims:** human relations; **Instructional Aims:** human relations; **Classroom Environment:** multicultural education; **School Practices:** ESL, parental involvement in school policy decisions, culturally diverse staff, community involvement in school policy decisions, strong school-community public relations effort, inservice teacher training in multicultural education, student involvement in curriculum planning, student involvement in school policy decisions, interracial student council, professionally staffed community relations office, ethnic studies curriculum; **Groups Studied:** African Americans, Arab Americans, Asian/Pacific Islander Americans, Hispanic (Latino/Chicano) Americans, Native Americans; **Elements Studied:** art, attitudes, beliefs, foods, history, kinship structure, language, literature, material culture, music, physical characteristics, religion, social customs, social structure; **Participating Disciplines:** English, foreign languages, humanities, language arts, social studies.

BROWARD COUNTY
Vilma T. Diaz
Director, Multicultural/Foreign Language
Ann Naves
Coordinator, Multicultural Curriculum
600 S.E. Third Avenue
Ft. Lauderdale, FL 33301
(305) 765-6680

Years In Operation: 4; **Grade Levels:** K-12; **Students Participating:** 178,060; **Community Participation:** use of community resources, use of human resources in the community, interaction with community organizations, advisory groups; **Social Goal:** single-group studies; **School Goal:** teaching the culturally different; **Primary Target:** all students; **Curricular Aims:** multicultural education; **Instructional Aims:** multicultural/social reconstructionist; **Classroom Environment:** multicultural/social reconstructionist; **School Practices:** transitional bilingual education, ESL, remedial classes, human relations training for teachers, inservice teacher training in multicultural education, Spanish as a second language, multilingual curriculum, Asian language(s), ethnic studies curriculum; **Groups Studied:** African Americans, Hispanic (Latino/Chicano) Americans, Native Americans, Caribbean Americans; **Elements Studied:** art, history, literature, music; **Participating Disciplines:** art, English, foreign languages, language arts, music, social studies; **Locally Produced Materials:** yes.

CHARLOTTE COUNTY
Pamela Steen
1520 Waterford Drive
Venice, FL 33948
(941) 255-0808

Grade Levels: K-12; **Students Participating:** 150; **Community Participation:** Parent Leadership Council; **Social Goal:** teaching the culturally different; **School Goal:** human relations; **Primary Target:** minority students; **Curricular Aims:** teaching the culturally different; **Instructional Aims:** multicultural/social reconstructionist; **Classroom Environment:** multicultural education; **School Practices:** ESL, human relations training for teachers, inservice teacher training in multicultural education.

CITRUS COUNTY
Dr. Thomas Curry
1007 West Main Street
Inverness, FL 34450
(904) 726-1931 ext. 242

COLLIER COUNTY

Maria Torres
Coordinator of LEP Programs
3710 Estey Avenue
Naples, FL 33942
(813) 436-6435

Years In Operation: 3; **Grade Levels:** K-12; **Students Participating:** 25,400; **Community Participation:** use of community resources, use of human resources in the community, study of the community, interaction with community organizations, Parent Advisory Council; **Social Goal:** multicultural education; **School Goal:** multicultural/social reconstructionist; **Primary Target:** all students; **Curricular Aims:** multicultural/social reconstructionist; **Instructional Aims:** multicultural/social reconstructionist; **Classroom Environment:** multicultural education; **School Practices:** ESL, remedial classes, culturally diverse faculty, parental involvement in school policy decisions, culturally diverse staff, community involvement in school policy decisions, strong school-community public relations effort, inservice teacher training in multicultural education, Spanish as a second language, student involvement in school policy decisions, interracial student council, professionally staffed community relations office, professionally staffed human relations team, student human relations council, multilingual curriculum, standard English as a second dialect, ethnic studies curriculum; **Groups Studied:** African Americans, Asian/Pacific Islander Americans, French Americans, Hispanic (Latino/Chicano) Americans; **Elements Studied:** art, attitudes, beliefs, body language, culture and personality, dialect, drama, foods, history, kinship structure, language, literature, music, religion, social customs, social organization, values; **Participating Disciplines:** art, English, foreign languages, humanities, language arts, reading, theater; **Locally Produced Materials:** yes.

DADE COUNTY

Hyacinth Johnson
Supervisor, Multicultural Programs
1500 Biscayne Boulevard, Rm. 239
Miami, FL 33132
(305) 995-1174

Years In Operation: 5; **Grade Levels:** K-12; **Students Participating:** 321,955; **Community Participation:** community involvement in curriculum planning, use of community resources, use of human resources in the community, a community based instructional program, study of the community, interaction with community organizations; **Social Goal:** multicultural education; **School Goal:** human relations; **Primary Target:** all students; **Curricular Aims:** multicultural education; **Instructional Aims:** multicultural/social reconstructionist; **Classroom Environment:** multicultural/social reconstructionist; **School Practices:** transitional bilingual education, ESL, remedial classes, culturally diverse faculty, parental involvement in school policy decisions, culturally diverse staff, human relations training for teachers, community involvement in school policy decisions, strong school-community public relations effort, inservice teacher training in multicultural education, student involvement in curricular planning, Spanish as a second language, student involvement in school policy decisions, interracial student council, human relations training for students, professionally staffed community relations office, bilingual curriculum, professionally staffed human relations team, student human relations council, bicultural curriculum, multilingual curriculum, standard English as a second dialect, Asian language(s), Native American language(s), ethnic studies curriculum; **Groups Studied:** African Americans, French Americans, German Americans, Hispanic (Latino/Chicano) Americans, Native Americans, Haitian Americans; **Elements Studied:** art, attitudes, beliefs, body language, culture and personality, dialect, drama, foods, history, kinship structure, language, literature, material culture, music, physical characteristics, religion, social customs, social organization, social structure, values; **Participating Disciplines:** art, business, English, foreign languages, health, home economics, humanities, industrial arts, language arts, mathematics, music, physical education, reading, science, social studies, theater; **Locally Produced Materials:** yes.

DUVAL COUNTY

Levi H. McIntosh, Jr.
Assistant Superintendent, Alternative Programs
1701 Prudential Drive
Jacksonville, FL 32207
(904) 390-2010

Grade Levels: K-12; **Students Participating:** 120,000; **Community Participation:** use of community resources, use of human resources in the community, interaction with community organizations; **Social Goal:** multicultural education; **School Goal:** human relations; **Primary Target:** all students; **Curricular Aims:** multicultural education; **Instructional Aims:** multicultural education; **Classroom Environment:** multicultural/social reconstructionist; **School Practices:** transitional bilingual education, ESL, culturally diverse faculty, culturally diverse staff, human relations training for teachers, community involvement in school policy decisions, strong school-community public relations effort, inservice teacher training in multicultural education, Spanish as a second language, interracial student council, bilingual curriculum, professionally staffed human relations team, bicultural curriculum, multilingual curriculum, standard English as a second dialect, ethnic studies curriculum; **Groups Studied:** African Americans, Arab Americans, Asian/Pacific Islander Americans, French Americans, German Americans, Greek Americans, Hispanic (Latino/Chicano) Americans, Iranian Americans, Irish Americans, Italian Americans, Native Americans, Portuguese Americans, Scandinavian Americans, Slavic Americans; **Elements Studied:** art, attitudes, beliefs, body language, culture and personality, dialect, drama, foods, history, kinship structure, language, literature, material culture, music, physical characteristics, religion, social customs, social organization, social structure, values; **Participating Disciplines:** art, business, English, foreign languages, health, home economics, humanities, industrial arts, language arts, mathematics, music, physical education, reading, science, social studies, theater; **Locally Produced Materials:** yes.

ESCAMBIA COUNTY
Sandra Riley
TOSA, Dropout Prevention
30 East Texas Drive
Pensacola, FL 32503
(904) 469-5318

Grade Levels: K-12; **Students Participating:** 30,000; **Community Participation:** community involvement in curriculum planning, use of community resources, use of human resources in the community, community based instructional program, study of the community, interaction with community organizations; **Social Goal:** human relations; **School Goal:** multicultural education; **Primary Target:** all students; **Curricular Aims:** multicultural education; **Instructional Aims:** multicultural education; **Classroom Environment:** multicultural/social reconstructionist; **School Practices:** ESL, remedial classes, culturally diverse faculty, parental involvement in school policy decisions, human relations training for teachers, community involvement in school policy decisions, inservice teacher training in multicultural education, student involvement in school policy decisions, interracial student council, human relations training for students, professionally staffed community relations office, ethnic studies curriculum; **Group Studied:** African Americans; **Elements Studied:** art, attitudes, beliefs, culture and personality, foods, language, music, religion, social structure, values; **Participating Disciplines:** art, English, foreign languages, language arts, music, reading, social studies; **Locally Produced Materials:** yes.

HILLSBOROUGH COUNTY
Ruth A. Hall
Supervisor, Multiethnic Programs
P.O. Box 3408
Tampa, FL 33601
(813) 272-4440

Grade Levels: K-12; **Students Participating:** 132,224; **Community Participation:** a community based instructional program, study of the community, interaction with community organizations; **Social Goal:** multicultural education; **School Goal:** multicultural education; **Primary Target:** all students; **Curricular Aims:** multicultural education; **Instructional Aims:** multicultural education; **Classroom Environment:** multicultural education; **School Practices:** parental involvement in school policy decisions, human relations training for teachers, inservice teacher training in multicultural education, human relations training for students, professionally staffed human relations team, ethnic studies curriculum; **Groups Studied:** African Americans, Asian/Pacific Islander Americans, Hispanic (Latino/Chicano) Americans, Native Americans, European Americans; **Participating Disciplines:** art, foreign languages, health, language arts, mathematics, music, physical education, reading, science, social studies; **Locally Produced Materials:** yes.

INDIAN RIVER COUNTY
Bonnie Swanson
Director of Instruction
1990 25th Street
Vero Beach, FL 32960
(407) 564-3067

LAKE COUNTY
Cheryl Bartesh
201 West Burleigh Boulevard
Tavares, FL 32788
(904) 343-3531

Years In Operation: 5; **Grade Levels:** K-12; **Students Participating:** 22,208; **Community Involvement:** community involvement in curriculum planning, use of community resources, use of human resources in the community, study of the community; **Social Goal:** human relations; **School Goal:** multicultural education; **Primary Target:** all students; **Curricular Aims:** multicultural/social reconstructionist; **Instructional Aims:** multicultural/social reconstructionist; **Classroom Environment:** multicultural education; **School Practices:** ESL, remedial classes, culturally diverse faculty, parental involvement in school policy decisions, culturally diverse staff, human relations training for teachers, community involvement in school policy decisions, strong school-community public relations effort, inservice teacher training in multicultural education, student involvement in curriculum planning, Spanish as a second language, professionally staffed community relations office; **Locally Produced Materials:** yes.

MANATEE COUNTY
Patrick G. Mullins
Specialist, Social Studies/Multicultural Ed.
P.O. Box 9069
Bradenton, FL 34206
(813) 741-7405

Years In Operation: 2; **Grade Levels:** K-12; **School Goal:** human relations; **Primary Target:** low achieving students; **Curricular Aims:** multicultural education; **School Practices:** ESL, remedial classes, culturally diverse faculty, parental involvement in school policy decisions, culturally diverse staff, human relations training for teachers, community involvement in school policy decisions, strong school-community public relations effort, inservice teacher training in multicultural education, Spanish as a second language, interracial student council, human relations training for students, student human relations council; **Locally Produced Materials:** yes.

OKALOOSA COUNTY

Pati Boyles
120 Lowery Place SE
Fort Walton, FL 32548
(904) 833-3109

Years In Operation: 4; **Grade Levels:** K-12; **Students Participating:** 28,177; **Community Participation:** community involvement in curriculum planning, use of community resources, use of human resources in the community, interaction with community organizations, School Advisory Council; **Social Goal:** human relations; **School Goal:** human relations; **Primary Target:** all students; **Curricular Aims:** multicultural/social reconstructionist; **Instructional Aims:** multicultural/social reconstructionist; **Classroom Environment:** multicultural/social reconstructionist; **School Practices:** ESL, remedial classes, culturally diverse faculty, parental involvement in school policy decisions, culturally diverse staff, human relations training for teachers, community involvement in school policy decisions, strong school-community public relations effort, inservice teacher training in multicultural education, Spanish as a second language, student involvement in school policy decisions, interracial student council, human relations training for students, bilingual curriculum, ethnic studies curriculum; **Group Studied:** African Americans; **Elements Studied:** art, culture and personality, drama, foods, history, literature, music, social customs, social organization, social structure; **Participating Disciplines:** social studies; **Locally Produced Materials:** yes.

ORANGE COUNTY

Javier Melendez
Sr. Director, Multicultural Services
P.O. Box 271
Orlando, FL 32802
(407) 849-3200 ext. 2994

Years In Operation: 9; **Grade Levels:** K-12; **Students Participating:** 118,000; **Community Participation:** use of community resources, study of the community, interaction with community organizations, advisory councils, task forces; **Social Goal:** teaching the culturally different; **School Goal:** human relations; **Primary Target:** all students; **Curricular Aims:** multicultural educations; **Instructional Aims:** multicultural education; **Classroom Environment:** single-group studies; **School Practices:** transitional bilingual education, ESL, culturally diverse faculty, parental involvement in school policy decisions, culturally diverse staff, human relations training for teachers, community involvement in school policy decisions, strong school-community public relations effort, inservice teacher training in multicultural education, Spanish as a second language, interracial student council, human relations training for students, professionally staffed community relations office, bilingual curriculum, professionally staffed human relations team; **Locally Produced Materials:** yes.

OSCEOLA COUNTY
Lissette Brizendine
817 Billbeck Boulevard
Kissimmee, FL 34744
(407) 870-4008

Years In Operation: 4; **Grade Levels:** K-12; **Students Participating:** 24,309; **Community Participation:** use of community resources, interaction with community organizations; **Social Goal:** human relations; **School Goal:** teaching the culturally different; **Primary Target:** all students; **Curricular Aims:** single-group studies; **Instructional Aims:** multicultural education; **Classroom Environment:** single-group studies; **School Practices:** ESL, culturally diverse faculty, human relations training for teachers, community involvement in school policy decision, strong school-community public relations effort, inservice teacher training in multicultural education, professionally staffed community relations office, ethnic studies curriculum; **Groups Studied:** African Americans, Hispanic (Latino/Chicano) Americans; **Elements Studied:** beliefs, culture and personality, foods, history, social customs, social organization, social structure; **Participating Discipline:** social studies.

PASCO COUNTY
Peter Kennedy
Supervisor of Special Programs
7227 Land O Lakes Boulevard
Land O Lakes, FL 34639
(813) 996-3600

Years In Operation: 4; **Grade Levels:** 6-12; **Students Participating:** 3,200; **Community Participation:** use of community resources, use of human resources in the community, interaction with community organizations; **Social Goal:** human relations; **School Goal:** human relations; **Primary Target:** all students; **Curricular Aims:** multicultural/social reconstructionist; **Instructional Aims:** multicultural education; **Classroom Environment:** multicultural/social reconstructionist; **School Practices:** ESL, culturally diverse faculty, community involvement in school policy decisions, strong school-community public relations effort, inservice teacher training in multicultural education, interracial student council, human relations training for students.

PINELLAS COUNTY
Lewis Williams
Associate Superintendent, Pupil Assignment & Human Relations
P.O. Box 2942
Largo, FL 34649-2942
(813) 588-6302

SAINT LUCIE COUNTY
Dr. Vanessa Parker
Coordinator, Human Relations & Diversity Training
1200 Delaware Avenue
Ft. Pierce, FL 34950
(407) 468-5140

Years In Operation: 2; **Grade Levels:** K-12; **Students Participating:** 27,000; **Community Participation:** use of human resources in the community, interaction with community organizations; **Social Goal:** multicultural education; **School Goal:** multicultural education; **Primary Target:** all students; **Curricular Aims:** single-group studies; **Instructional Aims:** multicultural/social reconstructionist; **Classroom Environment:** multicultural/social reconstructionist; **School Practices:** transitional bilingual education, ESL, culturally diverse faculty, parental involvement in school policy decisions, culturally diverse staff, human relations training for teachers, inservice teacher training in multicultural education, interracial student council, human relations training for students, professionally staffed community relations office, professionally staffed human relations team, multilingual curriculum, standard English as a second dialect, ethnic studies curriculum; **Groups Studied:** African Americans, Asian/Pacific Islander Americans, Hispanic (Latino/Chicano) Americans, Irish Americans, Italian Americans, Native Americans; **Elements Studied:** attitudes, beliefs, culture and personality, dialect, foods, history, kinship structure, language, material culture, music, physical characteristics, social customs, social organization, social structure, values; **Participating Disciplines:** humanities, language arts, reading, social studies; **Locally Produced Materials:** yes.

SANTA ROSA COUNTY
Gloria Bryan
Language Arts Coordinator
603 Canal Street
Milton, FL 32570
(904) 983-5045

Grade Levels: K-12; **Students Participating:** 17,364; **Community Participation:** use of community resources, use of human resources in the community, study of the community, interaction with community organizations; **Social Goal:** multicultural education; **School Goal:** multicultural education; **Primary Target:** all students; **Curricular Aims:** multicultural education; **Instructional Aims:** multicultural education; **Classroom Environment:** multicultural/social reconstructionist; **School Practices:** ESL, remedial classes, parental involvement in school policy decisions, culturally diverse staff, human relations training for teachers, community involvement in school policy decisions, strong school-community public relations effort, inservice teacher training in multicultural education, student involvement in curricular planning, student involvement in school policy decisions, interracial student council, human relations training for students.

SARASOTA COUNTY
Dr. Linda G. Thornton
Supervisor of Special State Programs
1960 Landings Boulevard
Sarasota, FL 34231
(813) 361-6450

Years In Operation: 5; **Grade Levels:** K-12; **Students Participating:** 560; **Community Participation:** interaction with community organizations; **Social Goal:** teaching the culturally different; **School Goal:** human relations; **Primary Target:** all students; **Curricular Aims:** multicultural education; **Instructional Aims:** multicultural education; **Classroom Environment:** human relations; **School Practices:** ESL, culturally diverse faculty, parental involvement in school policy decisions, human relations training for teachers, community involvement in school policy decisions, inservice teacher training in multicultural education, Spanish as a second language, interracial student council, professionally staffed human relations team, multilingual curriculum, ethnic studies curriculum; **Groups Studied:** African Americans, Asian/Pacific Islander Americans, Hispanic (Latino/Chicano) Americans, Slavic Americans; **Elements Studied:** attitudes, beliefs, body language, culture and personality, dialect, foods, social customs, social organization, social structure, values; **Participating Disciplines:** art, foreign languages, language arts, music, social studies, theater; **Locally Produced Materials:** yes.

VOLUSIA COUNTY
Dr. Betty Green
729 Loomis Avenue
Daytona, FL 32114
(904) 734-7190

Years In Operation: 5; **Grade Levels:** K-12; **Students Participating:** 2,000; **Community Participation:** Parent Leadership Council; **Social Goal:** human relations; **School Goal:** human relations; **Primary Target:** all students; **Curricular Aims:** multicultural education; **Instructional Aims:** multicultural/social reconstructionist; **Classroom Environment:** multicultural/social reconstructionist; **School Practices:** ESL, culturally diverse faculty, parental involvement in school policy decisions, culturally diverse staff, human relations training for teachers, community involvement in school policy decisions, inservice teacher training in multicultural education, Spanish as a second language, human relations training for students, professionally staffed community relations office, bicultural curriculum, multilingual curriculum, standard English as a second dialect, ethnic studies curriculum; **Groups Studied:** African Americans, Hispanic (Latino/Chicano) Americans, Native Americans; **Participating Disciplines:** English, foreign languages, language arts, social studies.

GEORGIA

Atlanta City
Patricia Guillory
Director, Social Studies and Pluralistic Curriculum
786 Cleveland Avenue SW
Atlanta, GA 30315
(404) 763-6782

Years In Operation: 1; **Grade Levels:** K-12; **Students Participating:** 54,000; **Community Participation:** community involvement in curriculum planning, use of human resources in the community, interaction with community organizations; **Social Goal:** multicultural education; **School Goal:** multicultural education; **Primary Target:** all students; **Curricular Aims:** multicultural education; **Instructional Aims:** multicultural education; **Classroom Environment:** multicultural/social reconstructionist; **School Practices:** parental involvement in school policy decisions, culturally diverse staff, human relations training for teachers, community involvement in school policy decisions, inservice teacher training in multicultural education, student involvement in school policy decisions, interracial student council, bicultural curriculum, multilingual curriculum; **Elements Studied:** attitudes, beliefs, dialect, history, language, literature, music, physical characteristics, religion, social structure, values.

Bibb County
Grace B. McCormick
Secondary Social Studies
484 Mulberry Street
Macon, GA 31201
(912) 765-8551

Years In Operation: 10; **Grade Levels:** 7-12; **Students Participating:** 14,000; **Community Participation:** use of community resources, use of human resources in the community, a community based instructional program, study of the community, interaction with community organizations; **Social Goal:** human relations; **School Goal:** human relations; **Primary Target:** all students; **Curricular Aims:** multicultural education; **Instructional Aims:** multicultural/social reconstructionist; **Classroom Environment:** multicultural education; **School Practices:** transitional bilingual education, remedial classes, parental involvement in school policy decisions, culturally diverse staff, human relations training for teachers, community involvement in school policy decisions, strong school-community public relations effort, inservice teacher training in multicultural education, student involvement in curriculum planning, Spanish as a second language, interracial student council, human relations training for students, professionally staffed community relations office, multilingual curriculum, ethnic studies curriculum; **Groups Studied:** African Americans, Asian/Pacific Islander Americans, French Americans, German Americans, Hispanic (Latino/Chicano) Americans, Italian Americans, Native Americans; **Elements Studied:** art, beliefs, culture and personality, foods, history, language, literature, material culture, music, physical characteristics, religion, social customs, social organization, social structure, values; **Participating Disciplines:** English, foreign languages, humanities, language arts, mathematics, music, physical education, reading, social studies, theater; **Locally Produced Materials:** yes.

CARROLL COUNTY
Alan Krieger
Director of Student Services
164 Independence Drive
Carrollton, GA 30117
(404) 832-3568

Years In Operation: 1; **Grade Levels:** K-12; **Students Participating:** 8,120; **Classroom Environment:** multicultural/social reconstructionist; **School Practices:** parental involvement in school policy decisions, human relations training for teachers, community involvement in school policy decisions, strong school-community public relations effort, inservice teacher training in multicultural education, student involvement in school policy decisions, interracial student council, ethnic studies curriculum; **Groups Studied:** African Americans, Asian/Pacific Islander Americans, Hispanic (Latino/Chicano) Americans, Native Americans; **Elements Studied:** art, attitudes, beliefs, culture and personality, drama, foods, history, literature, material culture, music, physical characteristics, religion, social customs, social organization, social structure, values; **Participating Disciplines:** art, English, humanities, social studies; **Locally Produced Materials:** yes.

CHATHAM COUNTY
Marva E. Harris
Administrative Coordinator, Multicultural Education
Massie Heritage Interpretation Center
207 East Gordon Street
Savannah, GA 31401
(912) 651-7022

Years In Operation: 3; **Grade Levels:** K-12; **Students Participating:** 34,711; **Community Participation:** community involvement in curriculum planning, use of community resources, use of human resources in the community, study of the community, interaction with community organizations; **Social Goal:** multicultural education; **School Goal:** multicultural/social reconstructionist; **Primary Target:** all students; **Curricular Aims:** multicultural/social reconstructionist; **Instructional Aims:** multicultural/social reconstructionist; **Classroom Environment:** multicultural/social reconstructionist; **School Practices:** transitional bilingual education, ESL, culturally diverse faculty, culturally diverse staff, strong school-community public relations effort, inservice teacher training in multicultural education, student involvement in curriculum planning, professionally staffed community relations office, bilingual curriculum.

CLARKE COUNTY

Kathryn H. Hug, Ph.D.
Associate Superintendent, Planning & Instructional Programs
500 College Avenue, P.O. Box 1708
Athens, GA 30603-1708
(706) 546-7721 ext. 215; FAX: (706) 369-1804

Years In Operation: 20; **Grade Levels:** K-12; **Students Participating:** 10,697; **Community Participation:** community involvement in curriculum planning, use of community resources, use of human resources in the community, study of the community, interaction with community organizations; **Social Goal:** human relations; **School Goal:** multicultural/social reconstructionist; **Primary Target:** all students; **Curricular Aims:** multicultural/social reconstructionist; **Instructional Aims:** multicultural/social reconstructionist; **Classroom Environment:** multicultural/social reconstructionist; **School Practices:** ESL, remedial classes, culturally diverse faculty, parental involvement in school policy decisions, culturally diverse staff, human relations training for teachers, community involvement in school policy decisions, strong school-community public relations effort, inservice teacher training in multicultural education, interracial student council, human relations training for students, professionally staffed community relations office, bicultural curriculum, ethnic studies curriculum; **Participating Discipline:** social studies; **Locally Produced Materials:** yes.

CLAYTON COUNTY

Robynn Greer
Coordinator for Social Studies, Secondary Education
Ann Martin
Coordinator for Social Studies, Elementary Education
2284 Old Rex-Morrow Road
Morrow, GA 30260
(404) 362-3800

COBB COUNTY

Sharon Hunt
Supervisor, Cultural Diversity Programs
P.O. Box 1088
Marietta, GA 30066
(404) 426-3379

Years In Operation: 4; **Grade Levels:** K-12; **Students Participating:** 80,000; **Community Participation:** community involvement in curriculum planning, use of com-

munity resources, use of human resources in the community, interaction with community organizations; **Social Goal:** multicultural/social reconstructionist; **School Goal:** multicultural/social reconstructionist; **Primary Target:** all students; **Curricular Aims:** multicultural/social reconstructionist; **Instructional Aims:** multicultural/social reconstructionist; **Classroom Environment:** multicultural/social reconstructionist; **School Practices:** transitional bilingual education, ESL, remedial classes, culturally diverse faculty, parental involvement in school policy decisions, culturally diverse staff, human relations training for teachers, community involvement in school policy decisions, strong school-community public relations effort, inservice teacher training in multicultural education, student involvement in curriculum planning, Spanish as a second language, student involvement in school policy decisions, interracial student council, human relations training for students, professionally staffed community relations office, bilingual curriculum, professionally staffed human relations team, student human relations council, Asian language(s), ethnic studies curriculum; **Groups Studied:** African Americans, Arab Americans, Asian/Pacific Islander Americans, French Americans, German Americans, Greek Americans, Hispanic (Latino/Chicano) Americans, Iranian Americans, Irish Americans, Italian Americans, Native Americans, Portuguese Americans, Scandinavian Americans, Slavic Americans; **Elements Studied:** art, attitudes, beliefs, body language, culture and personality, dialect, drama, foods, history, kinship structure, language, literature, material culture, music, physical characteristics, religion, social customs, social organization, social structure, values; **Participating Disciplines:** art, business, English, foreign languages, health, home economics, humanities, industrial arts, language arts, mathematics, music, physical education, reading, science, social studies, theater; **Locally Produced Materials:** yes.

COWETA COUNTY
Dr. Lucie Welzant-Hayden
P.O. Box 280
237 Jackson Street
Newnan, GA 30264
(404) 254-2800

Years In Operation: 5; **Grade Levels:** K-12; **Students Participating:** 11,288;**Community Participation:** community involvement in curriculum planning, use of community resources, use of human resources in the community, interaction with community organizations; **Social Goal:** multicultural education; **School Goal:** human relations; **Primary Target:** all students; **Curricular Aims:** teaching the culturally different; **Instructional Aims:** multicultural education; **Classroom Environment:** human relations; **School Practices:** ESL, remedial classes, parental involvement in school policy decisions, culturally diverse staff, human relations training for teachers, community involvement in school policy decisions, strong school-community public relations effort, inservice teacher training in multicultural education, student involvement in school policy decisions, interracial student council, human relations training for students, professionally staffed community relations office.

DE KALB COUNTY
Dr. John E. Carr
Instructional Coordinator
3770 North Decatur Road
Decatur, GA 30032
(404) 297-7439

Years In Operation: 5; **Grade Levels:** K-12; **Students Participating:** 82,000; **Community Participation:** use of community resources, use of human resources in the community, interaction with community organizations; **Social Goal:** multicultural education; **School Goal:** multicultural/social reconstructionist; **Primary Target:** all students; **Curricular Aims:** teaching the culturally different; **Instructional Aims:** multicultural education; **Classroom Environment:** multicultural education; **School Practices:** transitional bilingual education, ESL, parental involvement in school policy decisions, culturally diverse staff, human relations training for teachers, strong school-community public relations effort, inservice teacher training in multicultural education, Spanish as a second language, student involvement in school policy decisions, interracial student council, human relations training for students, professionally staffed community relations office, professionally staffed human relations team, ethnic studies curriculum; **Group Studied:** African Americans; **Elements Studied:** art, attitudes, beliefs, body language, culture and personality, foods, history, literature, physical characteristics, religion, social customs, social organization, social structure, values; **Participating Disciplines:** art, business, English, foreign languages, health, home economics, humanities, industrial arts, language arts, mathematics, music, physical education, reading, science, social studies.

FULTON COUNTY
Patricia Guillory
Director, Social Studies and Pluralistic Curriculum
786 Cleveland Avenue
Atlanta, GA 30315
(404) 763-6786

Years In Operation: 1; **Grade Levels:** K-12; **Students Participating:** 54,000; **Community Participation:** community involvement in curriculum planning, use of human resources in the community, interaction with community organizations; **Social Goal:** multicultural education; **School Goal:** multicultural education; **Primary Target:** all students; **Curricular Aims:** multicultural education; **Instructional Aims:** multicultural education; **Classroom Environment:** multicultural/social reconstructionist; **School Practices:** parental involvement in school policy decisions, culturally diverse staff, human relations training for teachers, community involvement in school policy decisions, inservice teacher training in multicultural education, student involvement in school policy decisions, interracial student council, bicultural curriculum, multilingual curriculum, Asian language(s), Native American language(s), ethnic studies curriculum; **Elements Studied:** attitudes, beliefs, dialect, history, language, literature, music, physical characteristics, religion, social structure, values.

MUSCOGEE COUNTY
Judy Nail
P.O. Box 2427
Columbus, GA 31902-2427
(706) 649-0500

HAWAII

Dr. Alan B. Ramos
English for Second Language Learners Program
(808) 396-2511
Josephine Pablo
Title VII Projects
(808) 396-2522
189 Lunalilo Home Road, 2nd Floor
Honolulu, HI 96825

IDAHO

IDAHO FALLS
Joel Lapray
Director of Federal Programs
690 John Adams Parkway
Idaho Falls, ID 83401
(208) 525-7554

Years In Operation: 21; **Grade Levels:** K-12; **Students Participating:** 300; **Community Participation:** community involvement in curriculum planning, use of human resources in the community, a community based instructional program, interaction with community organizations; **Social Goal:** teaching the culturally different; **School Goal:** multicultural education; **Primary Target:** minority students; **Curricular Aims:** teaching the culturally different; **Instructional Aims:** multicultural education; **Classroom Environment:** multicultural education; **School Practices:** ESL, remedial classes, culturally diverse faculty, parental involvement in school policy decisions, human relations training for teachers, inservice teacher training in multicultural education, Spanish as a second language.

ILLINOIS

EAST ST. LOUIS
Clarence Seckel
Curriculum Coordinator
1005 State Street
East St. Louis, IL 62201
(618) 583-8261

Years In Operation: 5; **Grade Levels:** K-12; **Students Participating:** 14,000; **Community Participation:** study of the community, interaction with community organizations; **Social Goal:** single-group studies; **School Goal:** human relations; **Primary Target:** all students; **Curricular Aims:** human relations; **Instructional Aims:** multicultural education; **Classroom Environment:** single-group studies; **School Practices:** inservice teacher training in multicultural education, multilingual curriculum, ethnic studies curriculum; **Groups Studied:** African Americans, Native Americans; **Elements Studied:** art, history, literature, music, social customs, social organization, social structure; **Participating Disciplines:** art, English, language arts, music, social studies; **Locally Produced Materials:** yes.

NAPERVILLE
Mary Ann Bobosky
Director of Community Relations
203 West Hillside Road
Naperville, IL 60540
(708) 420-6815
Don Schroeter, Chairman
Naperville Education Foundation
Multicultural Committee
Naperville, IL 60563
(708) 357-2755

Years In Operation: 3; **Grade Levels:** K-12; **Students Participating:** 17,000; **Community Participation:** use of community resources, use of human resources in the community, interaction with community organizations; **Social Goal:** single-group studies; **School Goal:** human relations; **Primary Target:** minority students; **Curricular Aims:** multicultural education; **Instructional Aims:** multicultural education; **Classroom Environment:** multicultural/social reconstructionist; **School Practices:** ESL, culturally diverse faculty, parental involvement in school policy decisions, community involvement in school policy decisions, strong school-community public relations effort, inservice teacher training in multicultural education, interracial student council, human relations training for students, professionally staffed community relations office, bilingual curriculum, ethnic studies curriculum; **Group Studied:** African

Americans; **Elements Studied:** dialect, history, kinship structure, literature, social customs, social organization; **Participating Disciplines:** foreign languages, language arts, social studies; **Locally Produced Materials:** yes.

SCHAUMBURG

Dr. Ngoc-Diep T. Nguyen
Director, Bilingual & Multicultural Programs
524 East Schaumburg Road
Schaumburg, IL 60194-3597
(708) 885-6728

SPRINGFIELD

Teresa Haley-Jackson
Diversity Specialist
Leroy A. Jordan, Director
Research, Assessment, and Development
1900 West Monroe
Springfield, IL 62704
(217) 525-3085

Years In Operation: 1; **Grade Levels:** K-12; **Students Participating:** 15,000; **Community Participation:** community involvement in curriculum planning, use of community resources, study of the community, interaction with community organizations; **Social Goal:** single-group studies; **School Goal:** human relations; **Primary Target:** all students; **Curricular Aims:** teaching the culturally different; **Instructional Aims:** teaching the culturally different; **Classroom Environment:** multicultural/social reconstructionist; **School Practices:** transitional bilingual education, ESL, culturally diverse faculty, parental involvement in school policy decisions, human relations training for teachers, strong school-community public relations effort, inservice teacher training in multicultural education, student involvement in curriculum planning, student involvement in school policy decisions, human relations training for students, professionally staffed community relations office, professionally staffed human relations team, ethnic studies curriculum; **Groups Studied:** African Americans, Hispanic (Latino/Chicano) Americans, Native Americans; **Elements Studied:** beliefs, culture and personality, history, literature, values; **Participating Discipline:** social studies.

INDIANA

ELKHART

Alma C. Powell
Assistant Director, Curriculum & Instruction
2720 California Road
Elkhart, IN 46514
(219) 262-5533

Years In Operation: 1; **Grade Levels:** K-12; **Students Participating:** 1,500; **Community Participation:** use of community resources, use of human resources in the community, interaction with community organizations; **Social Goal:** single-group studies; **School Goal:** multicultural education; **Primary Target:** all students; **Curricular Aims:** multicultural education; **Instructional Aims:** single-group studies; **Classroom Environment:** multicultural/social reconstructionist; **School Practices:** culturally diverse faculty, inservice teacher training in multicultural education, professionally staffed community relations office.

EVANSVILLE-VANDERBURGH

Rick Borries
Supervisor of Social Studies
7517 Taylor Circle
Evansville, IN 47715
(812) 435-8467

INDIANAPOLIS

Dr. Pat A. Browne
Director, African Centered Multicultural Education
1140 Dr. Martin Luther King Jr. Street
Indianapolis, IN 46260
(317) 226-4611

LAWRENCE TOWNSHIP

Duane Hodgin, Ph.D.
Assistant Superintendent, Educational Support Services
7601 East 56th Street
Indianapolis, IN 46226
(317) 546-4921; FAX: (317) 543-3534

Years In Operation: 4; **Grade Levels:** K-12; **Students Participating:** 13,500; **Community Participation:** community involvement in curriculum planning, use of community resources, use of human resources in the community, study of the community, interaction with community organizations; **Social Goal:** multicultural education; **School Goal:** multicultural education; **Primary Target:** all students; **Curricular Aims:** multicultural/social reconstructionist; **Instructional Aims:** multicultural/social reconstructionist; **Classroom Environment:** multicultural/social reconstructionist; **School Practices:** transitional bilingual education, ESL, remedial classes, culturally diverse faculty, parental involvement in school policy decisions, culturally diverse staff, human relations training for teachers, community involvement in school policy decisions, strong school-community public relations effort, inservice teacher training in multicultural education, Spanish as a second language, student involvement in school policy decisions, interracial student council, human relations training for students, professionally staffed community relations office, bilingual curriculum, professionally staffed human relations team, standard English as a second dialect, Asian language(s); **Locally Produced Materials:** yes.

MONROE COUNTY
David Frye
Assistant Superintendent
315 North Drive
Bloomington, IN 47408
(812) 330-7700

Years In Operation: 3; **Grade Levels:** K-6; **Students Participating:** 580; **Community Participation:** use of community resources, use of human resources in the community, study of the community, interaction with community organizations; **Social Goal:** human relations; **School Goal:** human relations; **Primary Target:** all students; **Curricular Aims:** multicultural education; **Instructional Aims:** multicultural/social reconstructionist; **Classroom Environment:** multicultural/social reconstructionist; **Locally Produced Materials:** yes.

NEW ALBANY-FLOYD COUNTY
Deborah Wesley
Facilitator for Multicultural and Special Projects
Roger Moody
Curriculum, Director of Learning
2813 Grant Line Road
New Albany, IN 47150
(812) 949-4200

Years In Operation: 1; **Grade Levels:** K-12; **Students Participating:** 11,119; **Social Goal:** multicultural/social reconstructionist; **School Goal:** multicultural/social reconstructionist; **Primary Target:** all students; **Curricular Aims:** multicultural/social reconstructionist; **Instructional Aims:** multicultural/social reconstructionist; **Classroom Environment:** multicultural education; **School Practices:** transitional bilingual education, culturally diverse faculty, parental involvement in school policy decisions, culturally diverse staff, human relations training for teachers, strong school-community public relations effort, inservice teacher training in multicultural education, interracial student council, professionally staffed human relations team, ethnic studies curriculum; **Groups Studied:** African Americans, French Americans, German Americans, Irish Americans, Native Americans; **Elements Studied:** art, attitudes, beliefs, culture and personality, foods, history, language, literature, music, religion, social customs, social organization, social structure, values; **Participating Disciplines:** art, English, foreign languages, language arts, music, reading, social studies.

PERRY TOWNSHIP

Max B. Oldham
Director of Instruction
1130 East Epler Avenue
Indianapolis, IN 46227
(317) 780-4208

Years In Operation: 3; **Grade Levels:** K-12; **Students Participating:** 11,500; **Community Participation:** community involvement in curriculum planning, use of community resources, use of human resources in the community; **Social Goal:** single-group studies; **School Goal:** human relations; **Primary Target:** all students; **Curricular Aims:** multicultural education; **Instructional Aims:** multicultural education; **Classroom Environment:** multicultural/social reconstructionist; **School Practices:** culturally diverse faculty, parental involvement in school policy decisions, culturally diverse staff, human relations training for teachers, community involvement in school policy decisions, inservice teacher training in multicultural education, interracial student council, human relations training for students, professionally staffed human relations team, ethnic studies curriculum; **Groups Studied:** African Americans, Asian/ Pacific Islander Americans, French Americans, German Americans, Greek Americans, Hispanic (Latino/Chicano) Americans, Italian Americans, Native Americans, Slavic Americans; **Elements Studied:** culture and personality, drama, foods, history, language, literature, music, religion, social customs; **Participating Disciplines:** English; **Locally Produced Materials:** yes.

SOUTH BEND COMMUNITY

Mary Pat Hatcher-Disler
Co-Chair, Valuing Diversity in Schools
(219) 282-4053
Maritza Robles
Co-Chair, Valuing Diversity in Schools
(219) 282-4150
635 S. Main St.
South Bend, IN 46614
(219) 282-4053

Years In Operation: 3; **Grade Levels:** K-12; **Students Participating:** 21,000; **Community Participation:** community involvement in curriculum planning, use of com-

munity resources, use of human resources in the community, study of the community, interaction with community organizations; **Social Goal:** human relations; **School Goal:** human relations; **Primary Target:** all students; **Curricular Aims:** human relations; **Instructional Aims:** multicultural education; **Classroom Environment:** multicultural/ social reconstructionist; **School Practices:** transitional bilingual education, ESL, remedial classes, parental involvement in school policy decisions, culturally diverse staff, human relations training for teachers, community involvement in school policy decisions, strong school-community public relations effort, inservice teacher training in multicultural education, student involvement in curricular planning, Spanish as a second language, student involvement in school policy decisions, interracial student council, professionally staffed community relations office, bilingual curriculum, ethnic studies curriculum; **Locally Produced Materials:** yes.

Wayne Township

Dr. Charles Payne
Consultant, Multicultural Education
1220 South High School Road
Indianapolis, IN 46241
(317) 243-8251 ext. 631

Years In Operation: 13; **Grade Levels:** K-12; **Students Participating:** 12,500; **Community Participation:** community involvement in curriculum planning, use of community resources, use of human resources in the community, interaction with community organizations; **Social Goal:** multicultural/social reconstructionist; **School Goal:** multicultural/social reconstructionist; **Primary Target:** all students; **Curricular Aims:** multicultural/social reconstructionist; **Instructional Aims:** multicultural/social reconstructionist; **Classroom Environment:** multicultural/social reconstructionist; **School Practices:** human relations training for teachers, community involvement in school policy decisions, strong school-community public relations effort, inservice teacher training in multicultural education, human relations training for students, professionally staffed community relations office, professionally staffed human relations team, student human relations council, multilingual curriculum; **Elements Studied:** art, attitudes, beliefs, body language, culture and personality, dialect, drama, foods, history, kinship structure, language, literature, material culture, music, physical characteristics, religion, social customs, social organization, social structure, values; **Locally Produced Materials:** yes.

IOWA

Cedar Rapids
Nelson Evans
Director of Instruction/Human Resources
(319) 398-2401
Pat Wilson
Program Facilitator, Eduactional Service Center
(319) 398-2500
346 2nd Avenue SW
Cedar Rapids, IA 52404

Council Bluffs Community
Ron Diimig
Supervisor, Student Services
12 Scott Street
Council Bluffs, IA 51503
(712) 328-6423

Years In Operation: 11; **Grade Levels:** K-12; **Students Participating:** 10,000; **Community Participation:** community involvement in curriculum planning, use of community resources, use of human resources in the community, a community based instructional program, interaction with community organizations; **Social Goal:** multicultural education; **School Goal:** multicultural education; **Primary Target:** all students; **Curricular Aims:** multicultural education; **Instructional Aims:** teaching the culturally different; **Classroom Environment:** multicultural education; **School Practices:** ESL, parental involvement in school policy decisions, human relations training for teachers, community involvement in school policy decisions, strong school-community public relations effort, inservice teacher training in multicultural education, Spanish as a second language, human relations training for students, multilingual curriculum, Asian language(s), Native American language(s).

Davenport
Henry Caudle
Principal, Lincoln Fundamental School
318 East 7th Street
(319) 324-0497
Dr. Daryl Spaans
Director of Schools
1001 Harrison Street
Davenport, IA 52803
(319) 323-9951

Des Moines Independent
Mary Lynne Jones
Director, Intercultural Programs
1800 Grand Avenue
Des Moines, IA 50309
(515) 242-7781

Years In Operation: 14; **Grade Levels:** K-12; **Students Participating:** 30,000; **Community Participation:** use of community resources, use of human resources in the community, interaction with community organizations; **Social Goal:** multicultural education; **School Goal:** multicultural education; **Primary Target:** all students; **Curricular Aims:** multicultural education; **Instructional Aims:** multicultural/social reconstructionist; **Classroom Environment:** multicultural/social reconstructionist; **School Practices:** transitional bilingual education, ESL, remedial classes, culturally diverse faculty, parental involvement in school policy decisions, culturally diverse staff, human relations training for teachers, community involvement in school policy decisions, strong school-community public relations effort, inservice teacher training in multicultural education, student involvement in curricular planning, student involvement in school policy decisions, interracial student council, human relations training for students, professionally staffed community relations office, bilingual curriculum, professionally staffed human relations team, bicultural curriculum, multilingual curriculum, ethnic studies curriculum; **Group Studied:** African Americans; **Elements Studied:** art, attitudes, beliefs, body language, culture and personality, dialect, drama, foods, history, kinship structure, language, literature, material culture, music, physical characteristics, religion, social customs, social organization, social structure, values; **Participating Discipline:** social studies; **Locally Produced Materials:** yes; **Materials Available for Purchase:** yes.

Sioux City Community
Roxanne Gould
Director, Educational Equity
(712) 279-6075
Patty Wells
Indian Education Specialist
(712) 279-6740
1221 Pierce Street
Eunice Barnes
Minorities in Teaching
1010 Iowa Street
(712) 279-6816
Caroline Donaway
ESL-Coordinator
1121 Jackson Street
(712) 279-6079
Sioux City, IA 51105

Years In Operation: 12; **Grade Levels:** K-12; **Students Participating:** 15,000; **Community Participation:** community involvement in curriculum planning, use of community resources, use of human resources in the community, interaction with community organizations, Educational Equity Committee; **Social Goal:** multicultural education; **School Goal:** multicultural education; **Primary Target:** all students; **Curricular Aims:** multicultural/social reconstructionist; **Instructional Aims:** multicultural/social reconstructionist; **Classroom Environment:** multicultural/social reconstructionist; **School Practices:** ESL, parental involvement in school policy decisions, culturally diverse staff, human relations training for teachers, inservice teacher training in multicultural education, interracial student council, human relations training for students, standard English as a second dialect, ethnic studies curriculum; **Elements Studied:** art, attitudes, beliefs, body language, culture and personality, dialect, drama, foods, history, kinship structure, language, literature, material culture, music, physical characteristics, religion, social customs, social organization, social structure, values; **Participating Disciplines:** art, business, English, foreign languages, home economics, humanities, industrial arts, language arts, mathematics, music, physical education, reading, science, social studies, theater; **Locally Produced Materials:** yes.

Waterloo Community
Ray Richardson
Associate Superintendent
1516 Washington Street
Waterloo, IA 50702
(319) 291-4842

KANSAS

KANSAS CITY
Christine Smith
Supervisor, Elementary Art & Multicultural Education
1620 South 21st Street
Kansas City, KS 66106
(913) 722-7373

OLATHE
Barbara Russell
Coordinator, Instructional Materials Center
14090 Black Bob Road
Olathe, KS 66062
(913) 780-7006

Years In Operation: 5; **Grade Levels:** K-12; **Students Participating:** 16,000; **Community Participation:** use of community resources, use of human resources in the community, community based instructional program, study of the community, interaction with community organizations; **Social Goal:** human relations; **School Goal:** human relations; **Primary Target:** all students; **Curricular Aims:** human relations; **Instructional Aims:** multicultural education; **Classroom Environment:** single-group studies; **School Practices:** ESL, remedial classes, human relations training for teachers, strong school-community public relations effort, inservice teacher training in multicultural education, Spanish as a second language, human relations training for students, professionally staffed community relations office, professionally staffed human relations team, student human relations council, ethnic studies curriculum; **Groups Studied:** African Americans, Asian/Pacific Islander Americans, Hispanic (Latino/Chicano) Americans, Irish Americans, Italian Americans, Native Americans; **Elements Studied:** art, attitudes, body language, culture and personality, drama, foods, history, language, literature, material culture, music, social customs; **Participating Disciplines:** art, English, foreign languages, humanities, language arts, music, social studies, theater.

TOPEKA
Sara Cocolis
Multicultural Education Coordinator
624 SW 24th Street
Topeka, KS 66611
(913) 233-0313

Wichita
Jan Davis
Executive Director of Diversity Development
201 North Water
Wichita, KS 67202
(316) 833-4701

Years In Operation: 1; **Community Participation:** use of community resources, interaction with community organizations; **Social Goal:** human relations; **School Goal:** multicultural education; **Primary Target:** all students; **Curricular Aims:** human relations; **Instructional Aims:** teaching the culturally different; **Classroom Environment:** multicultural/social reconstructionist; **School Practices:** transitional bilingual education, ESL, culturally diverse faculty, parental involvement in school policy decisions, culturally diverse staff, human relations training for teachers, community involvement in school policy decisions, strong school-community public relations effort, inservice teacher training in multicultural education, interracial student council, human relations training for students.

KENTUCKY

Boone County
Peggy Arnold
Director of Curriculum Services
8330 US 42
Florence, KY 41042
(606) 282-3326

Years In Operation: 10; **Grade Levels:** K-12; **Students Participating:** 57; **Community Participation:** use of community resources, use of human resources in the community, interaction with community organizations; **Social Goal:** teaching the culturally different; **School Goal:** teaching the culturally different; **Primary Target:** low achieving students; **Curricular Aims:** teaching the culturally different; **Instructional Aims:** multicultural education; **School Practices:** ESL, remedial classes, parental involvement in school policy decisions, inservice teacher training in multicultural education.

HARDIN COUNTY
Patricia Lindauer
Strategic Plan Facilitator
110 South Main Street
Elizabethtown, KY 42701
(502) 769-8804

Years In Operation: 1; **Grade Levels:** K-12; **Students Participating:** 13,000; **Community Participation:** community involvement in curriculum planning, use of community resources, use of human resources in the community, study of the community, interaction with community organizations; **Social Goal:** human relations; **School Goal:** human relations; **Primary Target:** all students; **Curricular Aims:** multicultural/social reconstructionist; **Instructional Aims:** multicultural/social reconstructionist; **Classroom Environment:** multicultural/social reconstructionist; **School Practices:** transitional bilingual education, ESL, remedial classes, parental involvement in school policy decisions, culturally diverse staff, community involvement in school policy decisions, strong school-community public relations effort, inservice teacher training in multicultural education, professionally staffed community relations office, professionally staffed human relations team, ethnic studies curriculum; **Group Studied:** African Americans; **Elements Studied:** art, attitudes, beliefs, foods, history, social customs; **Participating Discipline:** social studies.

JEFFERSON COUNTY
Sara Jo Hooper
Multicultural Education Specialist
P.O. Box 34020
Louisville, KY 40232-4020
(502) 485-3741

LOUISIANA

IBERIA PARISH
Kenneth Buller
Programmer of Title VII/Migrant Programs
1204 Lemaire Street
New Iberia, LA 70560
(318) 364-7641

Years In Operation: 4; **Grade Levels:** 4-8; **Students Participating:** 170; **Community Participation:** use of human resources in the community, community based instructional program, interaction with community organizations; **Social Goal:** single-group studies; **School Goal:** human relations; **Primary Target:** low achieving students; **Curricular Aims:** multicultural education; **Instructional Aims:** human relations; **Classroom Environment:** single-group studies; **School Practices:** ESL, remedial classes, culturally diverse faculty, parental involvement in school policy decision, culturally diverse staff, human relations training for teachers, inservice teacher training in multicultural education, student involvement in school policy decisions, interracial student council, multilingual curriculum, standard English as a second dialect, ethnic studies curriculum; **Groups Studied:** African Americans, Asian/Pacific Islander Americans, French Americans, Hispanic (Latino/Chicano) Americans; **Elements Studied:** attitudes, beliefs, culture and personality, foods, history, language, social customs, values; **Participating Disciplines:** English, language arts, social studies.

ORLEANS PARISH
Dr. Bobbie L. Stevenson
Associate Director of Curriculum
3510 Gen. DeGaulle Drive
New Orleans, LA 70114
(504) 365-8800

Years In Operation: 3; **Grade Levels:** K-8; **Students Participating:** 84,444; **Community Participation:** use of community resources, use of human resources in the community, interaction with community organizations; **Social Goal:** multicultural education; **School Goal:** multicultural education; **Primary Target:** all students; **Curricular Aims:** multicultural education; **Instructional Aims:** multicultural/social reconstructionist; **Classroom Environment:** multicultural/social reconstructionist; **School Practices:** transitional bilingual education, ESL, remedial classes, community involvement in school policy decisions, inservice teacher training in multicultural education, bilingual curriculum; **Elements Studied:** art, attitudes, beliefs, culture and personality, drama, foods, history, kinship structure, literature, music, physical characteristics, social customs, values; **Participating Disciplines:** art, English, foreign languages, humanities, language arts, mathematics, music, reading, social studies, theater.

OUACHITA PARISH
Mickey Jackson
Curriculum Director
100 Bry Street
Monroe, LA 71210
(318) 338-2215

VERNON PARISH
Dr. William Foster
Supervisor of Bilingual Education
201 Belview Road
Leesville, LA 71446
(318) 239-3401

MARYLAND

ANNE ARUNDEL COUNTY
Nancy M. Mann
Assistant Superintendent for Instruction
2644 Riva Road
Annapolis, MD 21401
(410) 222-5400

Years In Operation: 3; **Grade Levels:** K-12; **Students Participating:** 70,000; **Community Participation:** community involvement in curriculum planning, use of community resources, use of human resources in the community, interaction with community organizations; **Social Goal:** multicultural education; **School Goal:** human relations; **Primary Target:** all students; **Curricular Aims:** multicultural/social reconstructionist; **Instructional Aims:** multicultural education; **Classroom Environment:** multicultural education; **School Practices:** ESL, remedial classes, culturally diverse faculty, parental involvement in school policy decisions, culturally diverse staff, human relations training for teachers, community involvement in school policy decisions, strong school-community public relations effort, inservice teacher training in multicultural education, student involvement in school policy decisions, interracial student council, human relations training for students, professionally staffed community relations office; **Locally Produced Materials:** yes.

BALTIMORE CITY
Dr. Thomas DeLaine
Coordinator, Multicultural Education
200 East North Avenue, Rm. 326
Baltimore, MD 21202
(410) 396-8706

BALTIMORE COUNTY
Evelyn Chatmon
Assistant Superintendent, Equity & Staff Development
(410) 887-7559
Kim Whitehead
Supervisor, Multicultural Education
(410) 887-2444
6901 North Charles Street
Towson, MD 21204

CALVERT COUNTY

Victoria Diange
Supervisor of Staff Development
1305 Dares Beach Road
Prince Frederick, MD 20678
(410) 535-7219

Years In Operation: 1; **Grade Levels:** K-12; **Students Participating:** 13,000; **Social Goal:** multicultural education; **School Goal:** human relations; **Primary Target:** all students; **Curricular Aims:** multicultural education; **Instructional Aims:** multicultural education; **Classroom Environment:** multicultural education; **School Practices:** ESL, remedial classes, culturally diverse faculty, parental involvement in school policy decisions, culturally diverse staff, human relations training for teachers, community involvement in school policy decisions, strong school-community public relations effort, inservice teacher training in multicultural education, student involvement in curricular planning, Spanish as a second language, student involvement in school policy decisions, interracial student council, human relations training for students.

CARROLL COUNTY

Peggy Altoff
Social Studies Supervisor
Co-Chair, Multicultural Task Force
55 North Court Street
Westminster, MD 21157
(410) 751-3000

Years In Operation: 1; **Grade Levels:** K-12; **Students Participating:** 23,000; **Community Participation:** use of community resources, use of human resources in the community, interaction with community organizations; **Social Goal:** human relations; **School Goal:** teaching the culturally different; **Primary Target:** all students; **Curricular Aims:** human relations; **Classroom Environment:** single-group studies; **School Practices:** culturally diverse staff, community involvement in school policy decisions, strong school-community public relations effort, inservice teacher training in multicultural education, student involvement in curricular planning, student involvement in school policy decisions, interracial student council, professionally staffed community relations office.

Cecil County
John Abel
Supervisor of Social Studies & Foreign Languages
201 Booth Street
Elkton, MD 21921
(410) 996-5472

Years In Operation: 16; **Grade Levels:** K-12; **Students Participating:** 14,258; **Community Participation:** use of community resources, use of human resources in the community, study of the community, interaction with community organizations; **School Goal:** multicultural education; **Primary Target:** all students; **Curricular Aims:** multicultural/social reconstructionist; **Instructional Aims:** multicultural education; **Classroom Environment:** multicultural/social reconstructionist; **School Practices:** ESL, culturally diverse faculty, parental involvement in school policy decisions, community involvement in school policy decisions, student involvement in school policy decisions.

Frederick County
Joyce Harris
Staff Development Facilitator
7630 Hayward Road
Frederick, MD 21702
(301) 694-1322

Grade Levels: K-12; **Students Participating:** 29,297; **Community Participation:** use of human resources in the community; **Social Goal:** human relations; **School Goal:** multicultural education; **Primary Target:** all students; **Curricular Aims:** multicultural education; **Instructional Aims:** multicultural education; **Classroom Environment:** multicultural education; **School Practices:** ESL, remedial classes, culturally diverse faculty, human relations training for teachers, community involvement in school policy decisions, strong school-community public relations effort, inservice teacher training in multicultural education, Spanish as a second language; **Locally Produced Materials:** yes.

Harford County
Agnes Purnell
Supervisor of Equity & Cultural Diversity
45 East Gordon Street
Bel Air, MD 21014
(410) 638-4181

Howard County
Jacqueline Shulik
10910 Route 108
Ellicott City, MD 21042
(410) 313-6642

Years In Operation: 9; **Grade Levels:** K-12; **Students Participating:** 32,959; **Community Participation:** community involvement in curriculum planning, use of community resources, use of human resources in the community; **Social Goal:** human relations; **Primary Target:** all students; **Curricular Aims:** multicultural education; **Instructional Aims:** teaching the culturally different; **Classroom Environment:** teaching the culturally different; **School Practices:** ESL, culturally diverse faculty, parental involvement in school policy decisions, culturally diverse staff, human relations training for teachers, community involvement in school policy decisions, strong school-community public relations effort, inservice teacher training in multicultural education, student involvement in curricular planning, Spanish as a second language, student involvement in school policy decisions, interracial student council, human relations training for students, professionally staffed community relations office, professionally staffed human relations team.

Prince Georges County
Pamela Harris
Multicultural Education Specialist
Sasscer Administration Building
Equity Assurance Office
14201 School Lane
Upper Marlboro, MD 20772
(301) 805-2761

Saint Mary's County
Dr. Charles E. Ridgell III
Supervisor of Social Studies & Student Relations
Department of Instruction
Loveville, MD 20656
(301) 475-5511

Years In Operation: 13; **Grade Levels:** K-12; **Students Participating:** 13,327; **Community Participation:** community involvement in curriculum planning, use of community resources, use of human resources in the community, a community based instructional program, study of the community, interaction with community organizations; **Social Goal:** multicultural education; **School Goal:** multicultural education; **Primary Target:** all students; **Curricular Aims:** multicultural/social reconstructionist; **Instructional Aims:** multicultural/social reconstructionist; **Classroom Environment:** multicultural/social reconstructionist; **School Practices:** transitional bilingual education, ESL, remedial classes, culturally diverse faculty, parental involvement in school policy decisions, culturally diverse staff, human relations training for teachers, community involvement in school policy decisions, strong school-community public relations effort, inservice teacher training in multicultural education, student involvement in curriculum planning, Spanish as a second language, student involvement in school policy decisions, interracial student council, human relations training for students, professionally staffed community relations office, professionally staffed human relations team, student human relations council, standard English as a second dialect, ethnic studies curriculum; **Groups Studied:** African Americans, Arab Americans, Asian/Pacific Islander Americans, French Americans, German Americans, Greek Americans, Hispanic (Latino/Chicano) Americans, Irish Americans, Italian Americans, Native Americans; **Elements Studied:** art, attitudes, beliefs, culture and personality, dialect, drama, foods, history, kinship structure, language, literature, music, physical characteristics, religion, social customs, social organization, social structure, values; **Participating Discipline:** social studies; **Locally Produced Materials:** yes.

WASHINGTON COUNTY
Edward Koogle
Supervisor of Social Studies
P.O. Box 730, 820 Commonwealth Avenue
Hagerstown, MD 21741
(301) 791-4174

Years In Operation: 1; **Grade Levels:** K-12; **Students Participating:** 18,678; **Community Participation:** community involvement in curriculum planning, use of community resources, use of human resources in the community, a community based instructional program, study of the community, interaction with community organizations, multicultural task force; **Social Goal:** multicultural education; **School Goal:** teaching the culturally different; **Primary Target:** all students; **Curricular Aims:** multicultural education; **Instructional Aims:** human relations; **Classroom Environment:** single-group studies.

WICOMICO COUNTY
Sandra M. Prillaman
Director of Curriculum
P.O. Box 1538, 101 Long Avenue
Salisbury, MD 21801
(410) 742-5128

Years In Operation: 3; **Grade Levels:** K-12; **Students Participating:** 13,000; **Community Participation:** community involvement in curriculum planning, use of community resources, use of human resources in the community, interaction with community organizations; **Social Goal:** multicultural education; **School Goal:** multicultural education; **Primary Target:** all students; **Curricular Aims:** multicultural education; **Instructional Aims:** multicultural education; **Classroom Environment:** multicultural/social reconstructionist; **School Practices:** ESL, remedial classes, culturally diverse faculty, parental involvement in school policy decisions, culturally diverse staff, human relations training for teachers, community involvement in school policy decisions, strong school-community public relations effort, inservice teacher training in multicultural education, student involvement in school policy decisions, interracial student council, ethnic studies curriculum; **Groups Studied:** African Americans, Arab Americans, Asian/Pacific Islander Americans, Hispanic (Latino/Chicano) Americans, Native Americans; **Elements Studied:** art, attitudes, beliefs, body language, culture and personality, dialect, drama, foods, history, language, literature, material culture, music, physical characteristics, religion, social customs, social organization, values; **Participating Disciplines:** art, business, English, foreign languages, health, home economics, humanities, industrial arts, language arts, mathematics, music, physical education, reading, science, social studies; **Locally Produced Materials:** yes.

MASSACHUSETTS

BOSTON
Dr. Amanda Amis
Director of Curriculum & Instruction
26 Court Street
Boston, MA 02108
(617) 635-9400

BROCKTON
Benjamin Silva, Jr.
Director of Bilingual Education
43 Crescent Street
Brockton, MA 02401
(508) 580-7509

Years In Operation: 2; **Grade Levels:** K-12; **Students Participating:** 14,000; **Community Participation:** use of community resources, use of human resources in the community, interaction with community organizations; **Social Goal:** human relations; **School Goal:** multicultural education; **Primary Target:** all students; **Curricular Aims:** multicultural education; **Instructional Aims:** single-group studies; **Classroom Environment:** single-group studies; **School Practices:** culturally diverse faculty, parental involvement in school policy decisions, culturally diverse staff, human relations training for teachers, community involvement in school policy decisions, inservice teacher training in multicultural education, student involvement in school policy decisions, interracial student council, human relations training for students, bilingual curriculum, student human relations council; **Elements Studied:** social customs, values.

FALL RIVER

Albert Attar
Principal, BMC Durfee High School
360 Elfbree Street
Fall River, MA 02720
(508) 675-8100

Years In Operation: 6; **Grade Levels:** 9-12; **Students Participating:** 2,000; **Community Participation:** community involvement in curriculum planning, use of community resources, use of human resources in the community, interaction with community organizations; **Social Goal:** human relations; **School Goal:** multicultural/social reconstructionist; **Primary Target:** all students; **Curricular Aims:** human relations; **Instructional Aims:** multicultural/social reconstructionist; **Classroom Environment:** multicultural/social reconstructionist; **School Practices:** transitional bilingual education, ESL, remedial classes, parental involvement in school policy decisions, human relations training for teachers, community involvement in school policy decisions, strong school-community public relations effort, inservice teacher training in multicultural education, Spanish as a second language, professionally staffed community relations office, bilingual curriculum, professionally staffed human relations team, bicultural curriculum, multilingual curriculum, standard English as a second dialect, Asian language(s), Native American language(s), ethnic studies curriculum; **Groups Studied:** African Americans, Hispanic (Latino/Chicano) Americans; **Elements Studied:** art, attitudes, culture and personality, foods, history, religion, social customs, social structure, values; **Participating Disciplines:** art, English, home economics, language arts, mathematics, music, reading, social studies, theater; **Locally Produced Materials:** yes.

LAWRENCE

Janice Ryan
Assistant Principal, Arlington School
255 Essex Street
Lawrence, MA 01840
(508) 975-5926
Jackie Rapisardi
Principal, Kane North School
400 Haverhill Street
Lawrence, MA 01840
(508) 975-5953

LOWELL
Peter S. Stamas
Project Director
89 Appleton Street
Lowell, MA 01852
(508) 441-3728

Years In Operation: 20; **Grade Levels:** K-12; **Students Participating:** 14,800; **Community Participation:** community involvement in curriculum planning, use of community resources, use of human resources in the community, a community based instructional program, study of the community, interaction with community organizations; **Social Goal:** multicultural education; **School Goal:** multicultural education; **Primary Target:** all students; **Curricular Aims:** multicultural/social reconstructionist; **Instructional Aims:** multicultural/social reconstructionist; **Classroom Environment:** multicultural education; **School Practices:** transitional bilingual education, ESL, culturally diverse faculty, parental involvement in school policy decisions, culturally diverse staff, human relations training for teachers, community involvement in school policy decisions, inservice teacher training in multicultural education, Spanish as a second language, student involvement in school policy decisions, human relations training for students, bilingual curriculum, bicultural curriculum, multilingual curriculum, standard English as a second dialect; **Locally Produced Materials:** yes.

LYNN
Jan Brochenough
Director of Educational Equity
42 Franklin Street
Lynn, MA 01902
(617) 477-7384

NEW BEDFORD
Ray Letendre
Facilitator, Gomes School
286 South Second Street
New Bedford, MA 02740
(508) 997-4511 ext. 2432

Years In Operation: 10; **Grade Levels:** K-6; **Students Participating:** 750; **Community Participation:** community involvement in curriculum planning, use of community resources, use of human resources in the community, study of the community, interaction with community organizations; **Social Goal:** multicultural education; **School Goal:** human relations; **Primary Target:** all students; **Curricular Aims:** human relations; **Instructional Aims:** multicultural education; **Classroom Environment:** multicultural education; **School Practices:** transitional bilingual education, ESL, remedial classes, parental involvement in school policy decisions, culturally diverse staff, human relations training for teachers, community involvement in school policy decisions, strong school-community public relations effort, inservice teacher training in multicultural education, bilingual curriculum, standard English as a second dialect, ethnic studies curriculum; **Groups Studied:** African Americans, Asian/Pacific Islander Americans, Hispanic (Latino/Chicano) Americans, Native Americans; **Elements Studied:** art, attitudes, beliefs, culture and personality, dialect, drama, foods, history, language, literature, music, social customs, values; **Participating Disciplines:** art, home economics, language arts, mathematics, music, physical education, reading, science, social studies, theater; **Locally Produced Materials:** yes.

SPRINGFIELD

Shirin Selph
Multicultural Specialist
195 State Street
Springfield, MA 01102-1410
(413) 787-7276

Years In Operation: 1; **Grade Levels:** K-12; **Students Participating:** 24,000; **Community Participation:** use of community resources, use of human resources in the community, study of the community; **Social Goal:** multicultural/social reconstructionist; **School Goal:** multicultural/social reconstructionist; **Primary Target:** all students; **Curricular Aims:** multicultural/social reconstructionist; **Instructional Aims:** multicultural/social reconstructionist; **Classroom Environment:** multicultural/social reconstructionist; **School Practices:** transitional bilingual education, ESL, remedial classes, culturally diverse faculty, parental involvement in school policy decisions, culturally diverse staff, human relations training for teachers, strong school-community public relations effort, inservice teacher training in multicultural education, interracial student council, human relations training for students, Asian language(s), ethnic studies curriculum; **Groups Studied:** African Americans, Hispanic (Latino/Chicano) Americans, Native Americans; **Elements Studied:** art, attitudes, beliefs, culture and personality, foods, history, kinship structure, language, literature, music, physical characteristics, social customs, social organization, social structure, values; **Participating Disciplines:** art, foreign languages, home economics, humanities, music, reading, science, social studies, theater; **Locally Produced Materials:** yes.

WORCESTER
Antonio Fernandez
Quadrant Manager
(508) 799-3221
Stacey A. DeBoise
Affirmative Action Office
20 Irving Street
Worcester, MA 01609
(508) 799-3021

Years In Operation: 2; **Grade Levels:** K-12; **Students Participating:** 23,000; **Community Participation:** use of community resources, use of human resources in the community, study of the community, interaction with community organizations; **Social Goal:** single-group studies; **School Goal:** multicultural/social reconstructionist; **Primary Target:** all students; **Curricular Aims:** multicultural/social reconstructionist; **Instructional Aims:** teaching the culturally different; **Classroom Environment:** multicultural/social reconstructionist; **School Practices:** transitional bilingual education, ESL, remedial classes, culturally diverse faculty, parental involvement in school policy decisions, culturally diverse staff, human relations training for teachers, community involvement in school policy decisions, strong school-community public relations effort, inservice teacher training in multicultural education, Spanish as a second language, student involvement in school policy decisions, interracial student council, professionally staffed community relations office, bilingual curriculum, professionally staffed human relations team, standard English as a second dialect, Asian language(s), ethnic studies curriculum; **Groups Studied:** African Americans, Asian/ Pacific Islander Americans, Hispanic (Latino/Chicano) Americans; **Elements Studied:** art, culture and personality, foods, history, language, literature, music, social structure; **Locally Produced Materials:** yes.

MICHIGAN

DEARBORN CITY
Dr. Shereen Arraf
Coordinator of Bilingual & Compensatory Education
18700 Audelte
Dearborn, MI 48124
(313) 730-3028

Years In Operation: 20; **Grade Levels:** K-12; **Students Participating:** 3,000; **Community Participation:** community involvement in curriculum planning, use of community resources, use of human resources in the community, a community based instructional program, study of the community, interaction with community organizations, business partnerships; **Social Goal:** multicultural education; **School Goal:** multicultural/social reconstructionist; **Primary Target:** all students; **Curricular Aims:** multicultural education; **Instructional Aims:** multicultural education; **Classroom En-**

vironment: multicultural/social reconstructionist; **School Practices:** transitional bilingual education, ESL, remedial classes, culturally diverse faculty, parental involvement in school policy decisions, culturally diverse staff, community involvement in school policy decisions, strong school-community public relations effort, inservice teacher training in multicultural education, Spanish as a second language, student involvement in school policy decisions, interracial student council, human relations training for students, professionally staffed community relations office, bilingual curriculum, bicultural curriculum, Arabic languages, ethnic studies curriculum; **Groups Studied:** African Americans, Arab Americans, Hispanic (Latino/Chicano) Americans, Iranian Americans, Irish Americans, Italian Americans, Native Americans, Albanian Americans, Romanian Americans, Indian Americans; **Elements Studied:** art, attitudes, beliefs, body language, culture and personality, drama, foods, history, language, literature, music, religion, social customs, values; **Participating Disciplines:** art, business, health, language arts, music, reading, science; **Locally Produced Materials:** yes.

DETROIT

Dr. Felix Valbuena
Director of Office of Bilingual Education
5057 Woodward
Detroit, MI 48202
(313) 494-1075

Years In Operation: 5; **Grade Levels:** 3-12; **Students Participating:** 9,000; **Community Participation:** use of human resources in the community, study of the community; **Social Goal:** single-group studies; **School Goal:** human relations; **Primary Target:** minority students; **Curricular Aims:** multicultural education; **Instructional Aims:** multicultural education; **Classroom Environment:** human relations; **School Practices:** transitional bilingual education, ESL, human relations training for teachers, community involvement in school policy decisions, strong school-community public relations effort, bilingual curriculum, bicultural curriculum, multilingual curriculum, ethnic studies curriculum; **Groups Studied:** African Americans, Arab Americans, Asian/Pacific Islander Americans, Hispanic (Latino/Chicano) Americans; **Elements Studied:** culture and personality, history, social customs, social structure; **Participating Disciplines:** foreign languages, social studies; **Locally Produced Materials:** yes; **Materials Available for Purchase:** *Multicultural Awareness for the Classroom* (11 book series, including lesson plans and activities on national origin ethnic minorities).

FARMINGTON

Judith G. White
Assistant Superintendent, Instructional Services
32500 Shiawassee
Farmington, MI 48336
(810) 489-3327

Grand Rapids
Cathy Large
Facilitator of Multicultural Programs
1331 Franklin Street SE, P.O. Box 117
Grand Rapids, MI 49501-0117
(616) 771-2016

Kalamazoo
Kelly Sweet
Career Education & Social Studies Coordinator
1220 Howard Street
Kalamazoo, MI 49008
(616) 337-0168

Lansing
Dr. Melvin Villarreal
Associate Superintendent
519 West Kalamazoo
Lansing, MI 48933
(517) 374-4007

Years In Operation: 20; **Grade Levels:** K-12; **Students Participating:** 20,000; **Community Participation:** community involvement in curriculum planning, use of community resources, use of human resources in the community, interaction with community organizations; **Social Goal:** human relations; **School Goal:** multicultural education; **Primary Target:** all students; **Curricular Aims:** multicultural education; **Classroom Environment:** single-group studies; **School Practices:** transitional bilingual education, ESL, remedial classes, culturally diverse faculty, culturally diverse staff, human relations training for teachers, community involvement in school policy decisions, inservice teacher training in multicultural education, student involvement in curricular planning, Spanish as a second language, student involvement in school policy decisions, human relations training for students, Asian language(s), Native American language(s), ethnic studies curriculum; **Groups Studied:** African Americans, Asian/Pacific Islander Americans, Hispanic (Latino/Chicano) Americans, Native Americans; **Elements Studied:** art, attitudes, beliefs, culture and personality, foods, history, language, literature, material culture, music, social customs; **Participating Disciplines:** art, foreign languages, language arts, mathematics, music, reading, science, social studies; **Locally Produced Materials:** yes.

ROCHESTER COMMUNITY
Bev Stone
Assistant Superintendent for Instruction
501 West University
Rochester, MI 48307
(810) 651-6210

Years In Operation: 5; **Grade Levels:** K-12; **Students Participating:** 11,971; **Community Participation:** community involvement in curriculum planning, use of community resources, study of the community, interaction with community organizations; **Social Goal:** multicultural education; **School Goal:** multicultural education; **Primary Target:** all students; **Curricular Aims:** teaching the culturally different; **Instructional Aims:** human relations; **Classroom Environment:** human relations; **School Practices:** ESL, inservice teacher training in multicultural education, ethnic studies curriculum; **Groups Studied:** African Americans, Asian/Pacific Islander Americans, German Americans, Greek Americans, Hispanic (Latino/Chicano) Americans, Irish Americans, Italian Americans, Native Americans; **Elements Studied:** attitudes, beliefs, culture and personality, history; **Participating Discipline:** social studies.

SAGINAW
David J. Lutenski
Manager of Federal Programs
550 Millard
Saginaw, MI 48607
(517) 759-2283

Years In Operation: 25; **Grade Levels:** K-12; **Students Participating:** 13,500; **Community Participation:** community involvement in curriculum planning, use of community resources, use of human resources in the community, a community based instructional program, study of the community, interaction with community organizations; **Social Goal:** multicultural education; **School Goal:** teaching the culturally different; **Primary Target:** all students; **Curricular Aims:** teaching the culturally different; **Instructional Aims:** multicultural education; **Classroom Environment:** multicultural education; **School Practices:** transitional bilingual education, ESL, culturally diverse faculty, parental involvement in school policy decisions, culturally diverse staff, human relations training for teachers, community involvement in school policy decisions, strong school-community public relations effort, inservice teacher training in multicultural education, student involvement in school policy decisions, interracial student council, human relations training for students, professionally staffed community relations office, bilingual curriculum, professionally staffed human relations team; **Locally Produced Materials:** yes.

TRAVERSE CITY
Dr. Jayne Mohr
Assistant Superintendent
P.O. Box 32
Traverse City, MI 49684
(616) 922-6453

Years In Operation: 5; **Grade Levels:** K-12; **Students Participating:** 11,000; **Community Participation:** interaction with community organizations, community multicultural committee; **Social Goal:** human relations; **School Goal:** human relations; **Primary Target:** all students; **Curricular Aims:** multicultural/social reconstructionist; **Instructional Aims:** multicultural/social reconstructionist; **Classroom Environment:** multicultural/social reconstructionist; **School Practices:** transitional bilingual education, ESL, remedial classes, culturally diverse faculty, parental involvement in school policy decisions, culturally diverse staff, community involvement in school policy decisions, strong school-community public relations effort, inservice teacher training in multicultural education, student involvement in curricular planning, student involvement in school policy decisions, standard English as a second dialect.

WALLED LAKE
Dr. Jemil Metti
Bilingual/ESL Coordinator
695 North Pontiac Trail
Walled Lake, MI 48390
(810) 960-8391

Years In Operation: 5; **Grade Levels:** K-12; **Students Participating:** 450; **Community Participation:** community involvement in curriculum planning, use of community resources, use of human resources in the community, a community based instructional program, study of the community, interaction with community organizations; **Social Goal:** human relations; **School Goal:** multicultural education; **Primary Target:** all students; **Curricular Aims:** teaching the culturally different; **Instructional Aims:** multicultural/social reconstructionist; **Classroom Environment:** multicultural/social reconstructionist; **School Practices:** transitional bilingual education, ESL, strong school-community public relations effort, inservice teacher training in multicultural education, bilingual curriculum; **Elements Studied:** attitudes, beliefs, culture and personality, history, values; **Participating Disciplines:** foreign languages, language arts.

WAYNE-WESTLAND
Dr. Jane Kuckel
Assistant Superintendent for General Education
36745 Marquette
Westland, MI 48185
(313) 595-2010

Years In Operation: 1; **Grade Levels:** K-12; **Students Participating:** 15,000; **Community Participation:** community involvement in curriculum planning, use of community resources, use of human resources in the community, interaction with community organizations; **Social Goal:** human relations; **School Goal:** human relations; **Primary Target:** all students; **Curricular Aims:** single-group studies; **Instructional Aims:** teaching the culturally different; **Classroom Environment:** multicultural education; **School Practices:** culturally diverse faculty, parental involvement in school policy decisions, culturally diverse staff, community involvement in school policy decisions.

MINNESOTA

BLOOMINGTON
Coordinator of Diversity Education
8900 Portland Avenue South
Bloomington, MN 55420
(612) 885-8644

Years In Operation: 18; **Grade Levels:** K-12; **Students Participating:** 11,000; **Community Participation:** community involvement in curriculum planning, use of community resources, use of human resources in the community, a community based instructional program, interaction with community organizations; **Social Goal:** multicultural education; **School Goal:** human relations; **Primary Target:** all students; **Curricular Aims:** multicultural education; **Instructional Aims:** multicultural/social reconstructionist; **Classroom Environment:** multicultural/social reconstructionist; **School Practices:** ESL, remedial classes, culturally diverse faculty, parental involvement in school policy decisions, culturally diverse staff, human relations training for teachers, community involvement in school policy decisions, strong school-community public relations effort, inservice teacher training in multicultural education, interracial student council, human relations training for students, professionally staffed community relations office, student human relations council.

BURNSVILLE

Brenda Alston
Diversity Coordinator
600 East Hwy. 13
Burnsville, MN 55337
(612) 895-7279

Years In Operation: 1; **Grade Levels:** K-12; **Students Participating:** 11,000; **Community Participation:** community involvement in curriculum planning, use of community resources, use of human resources in the community, a community based instructional program, study of the community, interaction with community organizations; **Social Goal:** multicultural education; **School Goal:** multicultural/social reconstructionist; **Primary Target:** all students; **Curricular Aims:** multicultural/social reconstructionist; **Instructional Aims:** multicultural/social reconstructionist; **Classroom Environment:** multicultural/social reconstructionist; **School Practices:** transitional bilingual education, ESL, remedial classes, human relations training for teachers, strong school-community public relations effort, inservice teacher training in multicultural education, human relations training for students, standard English as a second dialect.

DULUTH

Mary Ann Lucas Houx
215 North 1st Avenue East
Duluth, MN 55802
(218) 723-4102

Grade Levels: K-12; **Students Participating:** 13,834; **Community Participation:** community involvement in curriculum planning, use of community resources, use of human resources in the community, community based instructional program, study of the community, interaction with community organizations; **Social Goal:** multicultural education; **School Goal:** multicultural education; **Primary Target:** all students; **Curricular Aims:** multicultural education; **Instructional Aims:** multicultural education; **Classroom Environment:** single-group studies; **School Practices:** ESL, remedial classes, culturally diverse faculty, parental involvement in school policy decisions, culturally diverse staff, human relations training for teachers, community involvement in school policy decisions, strong school-community public relations effort, inservice teacher training in multicultural education, human relations training for students, professionally staffed community relations office, professionally staffed human relations team, ethnic studies curriculum; **Groups Studied:** African Americans, Arab Americans, Asian/Pacific Islander Americans, French Americans, German Americans, Greek Americans, Hispanic (Latino/Chicano) Americans, Iranian Americans, Irish Americans, Italian Americans, Native Americans, Portuguese Americans, Scandinavian Americans, Slavic Americans; **Elements Studied:** art, attitudes, beliefs, body language, culture and personality, dialect, drama, foods, history, kinship structure, social customs, social organization, social structure, values, language, literature, material culture, music, physical characteristics, religion; **Participating Disciplines**: art, business, English, foreign languages, health, home economics, humanities, industrial arts, language arts, mathematics, music, physical education, reading, science, social studies, theater; **Locally Produced Materials:** yes; **Materials Available for Purchase:** Multicultural Gender Fair, Handicapped Aware Curriculum Guide.

MINNEAPOLIS
Cynthia Kelly
Coordinator, Multicultural Education
1215 NE Marshall Street
Minneapolis, MN 55413
(612) 627-2234

NORTH SAINT PAUL-MAPLEWOOD
Kathleen R. Huyen
Assistant Superintendent
(612) 770-4605
Sharon Cox
Director of Special Services
(612) 770-4752
2055 East Larpenteur Avenue
Maplewood, MN 55109

OSSEO
Etta Norwood
Cultural Specialist
11200 93rd Avenue North
Maple Grove, MN 55369
(612) 391-7099

Years In Operation: 5; **Grade Levels:** K-12; **Students Participating:** 20,000; **Community Participation:** use of community resources, interaction with community organizations; **Social Goal:** multicultural education; **School Goal:** multicultural education; **Primary Target:** all students; **Curricular Aims:** multicultural education; **Instructional Aims:** multicultural/social reconstructionist; **Classroom Environment:** multicultural/social reconstructionist; **School Practices:** inservice teacher training in multicultural education, ethnic studies curriculum; **Groups Studied:** African Americans, Asian/Pacific Islander Americans, Hispanic (Latino/Chicano) Americans, Native Americans; **Elements Studied:** history, literature, social customs, social organization, values; **Participating Discipline:** social studies; **Locally Produced Materials:** yes.

ROBBINSDALE

Jacqueline C. Fraedrich
Multicultural Coordinator
4148 Winnetka Avenue North
New Hope, MN 55427
(612) 536-3163

ROSEMOUNT

Essie Bronson
Multicultural/Diversity Coordinator
14445 Diamond Path Way
Rosemount, MN 55068
(612) 423-7840

Years In Operation: 1; **Grade Levels:** K-12; **Students Participating:** 25,000; **Community Participation:** use of community resources, use of human resources in the community, interaction with community organizations, site councils; **Social Goal:** multicultural education; **School Goal:** teaching the culturally different; **Primary Target:** all students; **Curricular Aims:** multicultural education; **Instructional Aims:** multicultural education; **Classroom Environment:** multicultural education; **School Practices:** ESL, culturally diverse faculty, parental involvement in school policy decisions, culturally diverse staff, community involvement in school policy decisions, inservice teacher training in multicultural education.

SAINT CLOUD

Art Dovman
Principal, Lincoln School
336 5th Avenue SE
St. Cloud, MN 56304
(612) 251-6343

Years In Operation: 4; **Grade Levels:** K-3; **Students Participating:** 380; **Community Participation:** use of community resources, use of human resources in the community, interaction with community organizations; **Social Goal:** multicultural education; **School Goal:** multicultural education; **Primary Target:** all students; **School Practices:** ESL, parental involvement in school policy decisions, human relations training for teachers, community involvement in school policy decisions, inservice teacher training in multicultural education, student involvement in school policy decisions; **Elements Studied:** art, culture and personality, drama, foods, history, literature, material culture, music, social customs.

SAINT PAUL
Carole Snyder
Associate Director of Curriculum
360 Colborne Street
St. Paul, MN 55102
(612) 228-3644

Grade Levels: K-12; **Students Participating:** 38,074; **Social Goal:** multicultural education; **School Goal:** multicultural education; **Primary Target:** all students; **Curricular Aims:** multicultural/social reconstructionist; **Instructional Aims:** multicultural education; **Classroom Environment:** multicultural education; **School Practices:** transitional bilingual education, ESL, parental involvement in school policy decisions, culturally diverse staff, community involvement in school policy decisions, inservice teacher training in multicultural education, bilingual curriculum, Native American language(s), ethnic studies curriculum; **Groups Studied:** African Americans, Asian/Pacific Islander Americans, Hispanic (Chicano/Latino) Americans; **Elements Studied:** art, beliefs, culture and personality, foods, history, language, literature, material culture, music, religion, social structure; **Participating Disciplines:** home economics, humanities, social studies; **Locally Produced Materials:** yes; **Materials Available for Purchase:** Native American Materials.

SOUTH WASH COUNTY
Dana Babbit
Principal
2665 Woodlane Drive
Woodbury, MN 55125
(612) 458-4325

Years In Operation: 3; **Grade Levels:** K-12; **Students Participating:** 13,500; **Community Participation:** community involvement in curriculum planning, use of community resources, use of human resources in the community, interaction with community organizations; **Social Goal:** multicultural education; **School Goal:** multicultural education; **Primary Target:** all students; **Curricular Aims:** multicultural/social reconstructionist; **Instructional Aims:** multicultural/social reconstructionist; **Classroom Environment:** multicultural education; **School Practices:** ESL, remedial classes, culturally diverse faculty, parental involvement in school policy decisions, culturally diverse staff, human relations training for teachers, community involvement in school policy decisions, strong school-community public relations effort, inservice teacher training in multicultural education, Spanish as a second language, interracial student council, Asian language(s).

MISSOURI

Columbia
Wanda E. Brown-Cox
Coordinator, Multicultural Education
Monica R. Naylor
Multicultural Education
555 Vandiver, Suite A
Columbia, MO 65202
(314) 886-2982; FAX: (314) 886-2160

Years In Operation: 3; **Grade Levels:** K-12; **Students Participating:** 15,000; relations; **Community Participation:** community involvement in curriculum planning, use of community resources, use of human resources in the community, interaction with community organizations; **Social Goal:** human relations; **School Goal:** human relations; **Primary Target:** all students; **Curricular Aims:** human relations; **Instructional Aims:** teaching the culturally different; **Classroom Environment:** multicultural/ social reconstructionist; **School Practices:** transitional bilingual education, ESL, remedial classes, human relations training for teachers, strong school-community public relations effort, inservice teacher training in multicultural education, ethnic studies curriculum; **Elements Studied:** art, foods, literature, music; **Participating Disciplines:** art, business, English, foreign languages, health, home economics, humanities, industrial arts, language arts, mathematics, music, physical education, reading, science, social studies, theater.

Ferguson-Florissant
Terry Reger
Social Studies Coordinator
1005 Waterford Drive
Florissant, MO 63033
(314) 831-4411

Years In Operation: 7; **Grade Levels:** K-12; **Community Participation:** use of community resources, use of human resources in the community, interaction with community organizations; **Social Goal:** multicultural education; **School Goal:** multicultural education; **Primary Target:** all students; **Curricular Aims:** multicultural education; **Instructional Aims:** multicultural education; **Classroom Environment:** multicultural education; **School Practices:** culturally diverse faculty, parental involvement in school policy decisions, human relations training for teachers, community involvement in school policy decisions, strong school-community public relations effort, inservice teacher training in multicultural education, human relations training for students, professionally staffed community relations office, ethnic studies curriculum; **Groups Studied:** African Americans, Asian/Pacific Islander Americans, French Americans, German Americans, Greek Americans, Hispanic (Latino/Chicano) Americans, Irish Americans, Italian Americans, Native Americans, Portuguese Americans; **Elements Studied:** art, attitudes, beliefs, culture and personality, drama, foods, history, kinship structure, language, literature, music, religion, social customs, social organization, social structure, values; **Participating Disciplines:** art, English, foreign languages, humanities, language arts, music, social studies; **Locally Produced Materials:** yes; **Materials Available for Purchase:** yes.

HAZELWOOD

Herb Kranze
Social Studies Consultant
15955 New Halls Ferry Road
Florissant, MO 63031-1298
(314) 839-9467

INDEPENDENCE

Marcia Haskin
Assistant Superintendent
1231 South Windsor
Independence, MO 64055
(816) 833-3433

Years In Operation: 6; **Grade Levels:** 3-12; **Students Participating:** 5,000; **Community Participation:** use of community resources, study of the community, interaction with community organizations; **Social Goal:** human relations; **School Goal:** human relations; **Primary Target:** all students; **Curricular Aims:** human relations; **Instructional Aims:** multicultural education; **Classroom Environment:** multicultural education; **School Practices:** ESL, remedial classes, parental involvement in school policy decisions, human relations training for teachers, community involvement in school policy decisions, strong school-community public relations effort, inservice teacher training in multicultural education, student involvement in school policy decisions, professionally staffed community relations office, professionally staffed human relations team, multilingual curriculum, Asian language(s).

KANSAS CITY

Jackie Baston
Instructional Specialist, Equity Education
1211 McGee Street
Kansas City, MO 64106
(816) 871-6334

LEE'S SUMMIT

Kay Baker
Assistant Superintendent, Elementary Instruction
Paul Munsen
Assistant Superintendent, Secondary Education
600 SE Miller Street
Lee's Summit, MO 64063
(816) 524-3368

Years In Operation: 3; **Grade Levels:** K-12; **Students Participating:** 11,000; **Community Participation:** community involvement in curriculum planning, use of community resources; **Social Goal:** human relations; **School Goal:** human relations; **Primary Target:** all students; **Curricular Aims:** single-group studies; **Instructional Aims:** multicultural education; **Classroom Environment:** multicultural education; **School Practices:** transitional bilingual education, ESL, human relations training for teachers, community involvement in school policy decisions, strong school-community public relations effort, inservice teacher training in multicultural education, Spanish as a second language, interracial student council, professionally staffed community relations office, bilingual curriculum, professionally staffed human relations team, standard English as a second dialect, ethnic studies curriculum; **Groups Studied:** African Americans, Asian/Pacific Islander Americans, Hispanic (Latino/Chicano) Americans; **Elements Studied:** art, attitudes, beliefs, body language, culture and personality, dialect, drama, foods, history, language, literature, music, physical characteristics, social customs, social organization, social structure, values; **Participating Disciplines:** art, English, foreign languages, home economics, humanities, language arts, music, physical education, reading, social studies; **Locally Produced Materials:** yes.

MEHLVILLE

Dr. Marvin Anthony
Voluntary Transfer Program
3120 Lemay Ferry Road
St. Louis, MO 63125
(314) 892-5000

Years In Operation: 2; **Grade Levels:** 1-12; **Community Participation:** use of human resources in the community; **Social Goal:** human relations; **School Goal:** multicultural education; **Primary Target:** minority students; **Curricular Aims:** multicultural education; **Instructional Aims:** multicultural education; **Classroom Environment:** human relations; **School Practices:** human relations training for teachers, inservice teacher training in multicultural education, interracial student council, human relations training for students.

Parkway
Dr. Paul Delanty
12657 Fee Fee Road
St. Louis, MO 63146
(314) 851-8100

Years In Operation: 11; **Grade Levels:** K-12; **Students Participating:** 9,066; **Community Participation:** community involvement in curriculum planning, use of community resources, use of human resources in the community, study of the community; **Social Goal:** multicultural education; **School Goal:** multicultural education; **Primary Target:** minority students; **Curricular Aims:** multicultural/social reconstructionist; **Instructional Aims:** multicultural education; **Classroom Environment:** multicultural/ social reconstructionist; **School Practices:** ESL, remedial classes, inservice teacher training in multicultural education, Spanish as a second language, interracial student council, professionally staffed community relations office, bilingual curriculum, student human relations council; **Elements Studied:** art, literature, music, social customs; **Participating Disciplines:** art, business, English, foreign languages, health, home economics, humanities, industrial arts, language arts, mathematics, music, physical education, reading, science, social studies, theater; **Locally Produced Materials:** yes.

Rockwood
Irene J. Hopkins
Curriculum Integration Program
16025 Clayton Road
Ellisville, MO 63011
(314) 391-2330

Years In Operation: 4; **Grade Levels:** K-12; **Students Participating:** 19,610; **Community Participation:** use of community resources, use of human resources in the community, interaction with community organizations; **Social Goal:** human relations; **School Goal:** human relations; **Primary Target:** all students; **Curricular Aims:** multicultural education; **Instructional Aims:** multicultural education; **Classroom Environment:** multicultural education; **School Practices:** ESL, remedial classes, culturally diverse faculty, culturally diverse staff, human relations training for teachers, community involvement in school policy decisions, strong school-community public relations effort, inservice teacher training in multicultural education, student involvement in curriculum planning, human relations training for students, professionally staffed community relations office; **Locally Produced Materials:** yes.

St. Joseph
Kay Medsker
Principal, Ellison School
Route 1
St. Joseph, MO 64507
(816) 667-5316

Years In Operation: 1; **Grade Levels:** K-6; **Students Participating:** 360; **Community Participation:** use of community resources, use of human resources in the community, interaction with community organizations; **Social Goal:** human relations; **School Goal:** multicultural education; **Primary Target:** all students; **Curricular Aims:** multicultural education; **Instructional Aims:** multicultural education; **Classroom Environment:** multicultural/social reconstructionist; **School Practices:** community involvement in school policy decisions, strong school-community public relations effort, inservice teacher training in multicultural education, Spanish as a second language, student involvement in school policy decisions, ethnic studies curriculum; **Groups Studied:** African Americans, Asian/Pacific Islander Americans, Hispanic (Latino/Chicano) Americans, Native Americans; **Elements Studied:** art, beliefs, foods, history, language, literature, music, social customs, social organization, social structure; **Participating Disciplines:** art, English, foreign languages, language arts, mathematics, music, physical education, reading, science, social studies.

St. Louis City
Benjamin M. Price
Executive Director of Curriculum & Staff
Madeleine Schmitt
Social Studies Supervisor
450 Desperes Avenue
St. Louis, MO 63112
(314) 863-7266 ext. 128

Years In Operation: 21; **Grade Levels:** K-12; **Students Participating:** 42,000; **Community Participation:** community involvement in curriculum planning, use of community resources, use of human resources in the community, a community based instructional program, study of the community, interaction with community organizations; **Social Goal:** multicultural education; **School Goal:** multicultural education; **Primary Target:** all students; **Curricular Aims:** multicultural/social reconstructionist; **Instructional Aims:** multicultural/social reconstructionist; **Classroom Environment:** multicultural education; **School Practices:** transitional bilingual education, ESL, culturally diverse faculty, parental involvement in school policy decisions, culturally diverse staff, community involvement in school policy decisions, strong school-community public relations effort, inservice teacher training in multicultural education, student involvement in school policy decisions, interracial student council, human relations training for students, professionally staffed community relations office, multilingual curriculum, ethnic studies curriculum; **Groups Studied:** African Americans, Asian/Pacific Islander Americans, French Americans, German Americans, Hispanic

(Latino/Chicano) Americans, Irish Americans, Italian Americans, Native Americans; **Elements Studied:** art, attitudes, beliefs, culture and personality, drama, foods, history, language, literature, music, religion, social customs, social organization, social structure, values; **Participating Disciplines:** art, business, English, foreign languages, health, home economics, humanities, industrial arts, language arts, mathematics, music, physical education, reading, science, social studies, theater.

NEBRASKA

LINCOLN
Radious Y. Guess
Multicultural Education Program
5901 O Street
P.O. Box 82889
Lincoln, NE 68501-2889
(402) 436-1604

Years In Operation: 23; **Grade Levels:** K-12; **Students Participating:** 30,000; **Community Participation:** community involvement in curriculum planning, use of community resources, use of human resources in the community, a community based instructional program, interaction with community organizations; **Social Goal:** multicultural/social reconstructionist; **School Goal:** multicultural education; **Primary Target:** all students; **Curricular Aims:** multicultural/social reconstructionist; **Instructional Aims:** multicultural/social reconstructionist; **Classroom Environment:** multicultural /social reconstructionist; **School Practices:** culturally diverse faculty, parental involvement in school policy decisions, culturally diverse staff, human relations training for teachers, community involvement in school policy decisions, strong school-community public relations effort, inservice teacher training in multicultural education, student involvement in curriculum planning, student involvement in school policy decisions, interracial student council, human relations training for students, professionally staffed community relations office, professionally staffed human relations team, student human relations council, bicultural curriculum, ethnic studies curriculum; **Groups Studied:** African Americans, Asian/Pacific Islander Americans, Hispanic (Latino/Chicano) Americans, Native Americans; **Elements Studied:** art, attitudes, beliefs, body language, culture and personality, dialect, drama, foods, history, kinship structure, language, literature, material culture, music, physical characteristics, religion, social customs, social organization, social structure, values; **Participating Disciplines:** English, home economics, language arts, music, reading, social studies; **Locally Produced Materials:** yes.

OMAHA
Dr. Joseph P. Gaughan
Assistant Superintendent/Instructional & Special Education
3215 Cuming Street
Omaha, NE 68131
(402) 557-2400

Years In Operation: 12; **Grade Levels:** K-12; **Students Participating:** 42,500; **Community Participation:** community involvement in curriculum planning, use of community resources, use of human resources in the community, study of the community, interaction with community organizations; **Social Goal:** single-group studies; **School Goal:** multicultural education; **Primary Target:** all students; **Curricular Aims:** multicultural education; **Instructional Aims:** multicultural/social reconstructionist; **School Practices:** transitional bilingual education, culturally diverse faculty, parental involvement in school policy decisions, culturally diverse staff, human relations training for teachers, community involvement in school policy decisions, strong school-community public relations effort, inservice teacher training in multicultural education, student involvement in curriculum planning, Spanish as a second language, student involvement in school policy decisions, interracial student council, human relations training for students, professionally staffed community relations office, bilingual curriculum, professionally staffed human relations team, bicultural curriculum, Asian language(s), ethnic studies curriculum; **Groups Studied:** African Americans, Hispanic (Latino/Chicano) Americans; **Elements Studied:** art, attitudes, beliefs, culture and personality, dialect, drama, foods, history, kinship structure, language, literature, material culture, music, physical characteristics, religion, social customs, social organization, social structure, values; **Participating Disciplines:** art, business, English, foreign languages, health, home economics, humanities, industrial arts, language arts, mathematics, music, physical education, reading, science, social studies, theater; **Locally Produced Materials:** yes.

NEVADA

CLARK COUNTY
Karla McComb
Assistant Director, Multicultural Education
601 North Ninth Street
Las Vegas, NV 89101
(702) 799-8444

Years In Operation: 3; **Grade Levels:** K-12; **Students Participating:** 165,000; **Community Participation:** community involvement in curriculum planning, use of community resources, use of human resources in the community, study of the community, interaction with community organizations, multicultural advisory committee; **Social Goal:** human relations; **School Goal:** multicultural education; **Primary Target:** all students; **Curricular Aims:** multicultural/social reconstructionist; **Instructional Aims:**

multicultural /social reconstructionist; **Classroom Environment:** multicultural/social reconstructionist; **School Practices:** transitional bilingual education, ESL, culturally diverse faculty, parental involvement in school policy decisions, culturally diverse staff, human relations training for teachers, community involvement in school policy decisions, strong school-community public relations effort, inservice teacher training in multicultural education, Spanish as a second language, student involvement in school policy decisions, interracial student council, human relations training for students, professionally staffed community relations office, professionally staffed human relations team, ethnic studies curriculum; **Group Studied:** African Americans; **Elements Studied:** art, attitudes, beliefs, culture and personality, foods, history, kinship structure, literature, music, social customs, social organization; **Participating Discipline:** social studies; **Locally Produced Materials:** yes; **Materials Available for Purchase:** Nevada curriculum on the holocaust.

WASHOE COUNTY
Jerry Holloway
Curriculum Coordinator
425 East 9th Street
Reno, NV 89520
(702) 851-5640

Years In Operation: 20; **Grade Levels:** K-12; **Students Participating:** 45,752; **Community Participation:** use of community resources, use of human resources in the community, interaction with community organizations; **Social Goal:** single-group studies; **School Goal:** human relations; **Primary Target:** all students; **Curricular Aims:** human relations; **Instructional Aims:** multicultural education; **Classroom Environment:** multicultural/social reconstructionist; **School Practices:** ESL, human relations training for teachers, community involvement in school policy decisions, strong school-community public relations effort, inservice teacher training in multicultural education, human relations training for students, professionally staffed community relations office; **Elements Studied:** attitudes, beliefs, culture and personality, foods, music, social customs, values; **Participating Disciplines:** English, foreign languages, language arts, music, reading, social studies; **Locally Produced Materials:** yes.

NEW HAMPSHIRE

MANCHESTER
196 Bridge Street
Manchester, NH 03104
(603) 624-6300

Years In Operation: 14; **Grade Levels:** 7-12; **Students Participating:** 150; **Community Participation:** use of community resources, use of human resources in the community, interaction with community organizations; **Social Goal:** teaching the culturally different; **School Goal:** teaching the culturally different; **Primary Target:** minority students; **Curricular Aims:** teaching the culturally different; **Instructional Aims:** teaching the culturally different; **Classroom Environment:** multicultural/social reconstructionist; **School Practices:** ESL, strong school-community public relations effort, inservice teacher training in multicultural education, Spanish as a second language.

NEW JERSEY

EAST ORANGE
Dr. Robert Penna
Director of Secondary Education
715 Park Avenue
East Orange, NJ 07017
(201) 266-5682

EDISON
Robert Panta
Assistant Superintendent
Cultural Understanding Initiative
100 Municipal Boulevard
Edison, NJ 08817
(908) 287-4400 ext. 215

Years In Operation: 1; **Grade Level:** 5; **Students Participating:** 950; **Community Participation:** community involvement in curriculum planning, use of human resources in the community; **Social Goal:** human relations; **School Goal:** human relations; **Primary Target:** all students; **Curricular Aims:** teaching the culturally different; **Instructional Aims:** human relations; **Classroom Environment:** human relations; **School Practices:** include all student groups in school activities; **Locally Produced Materials:** yes; **Materials Available for Purchase:** yes.

ELIZABETH CITY
Joseph Scuderi
Supervisor, Social Studies
27 Prince Street
Elizabeth, NJ 07208
(908) 558-3044

Years In Operation: 4; **Grade Levels:** K-12; **Students Participating:** 14,000; **Community Participation:** community involvement in curriculum planning, use of community resources, use of human resources in the community, study of the community, interaction with community organizations; **Social Goal:** multicultural education;

School Goal: human relations; **Primary Target:** all students; **Curricular Aims:** teaching the culturally different; **Instructional Aims:** multicultural/social reconstructionist; **Classroom Environment:** single-group studies, human relations; **School Practices:** transitional bilingual education, ESL, parental involvement in school policy decisions, culturally diverse staff, human relations training for teachers, community involvement in school policy decisions, strong school-community public relations effort, inservice teacher training in multicultural education, Spanish as a second language, human relations training for students, bilingual curriculum, ethnic studies curriculum; **Group Studied:** African American; **Elements Studied:** art, foods, history, literature, music, religion, social customs, social organization, social structure, values; **Participating Disciplines:** art, English, language arts, music, reading, social studies; **Locally Produced Materials:** yes.

HAMILTON TOWNSHIP
Saula Cutter
Consultant for Multicultural Education & Affirmative Action
90 Park Avenue
Hamilton Square, NJ 08690
(609) 890-3139

JERSEY CITY
Roy Beeler
Joint Activities Program
(201) 915-6960
Elaine Gardner
District Supervisor, Multicultural Studies
(201) 915-6073
Magda Savino
District Supervisor, Bilingual/ESL/World Languages
(201) 915-6145
346 Claremont Avenue
Jersey City, NJ 07305

Years In Operation: 15; **Grade Levels:** 4-7,11, 12; **Students Participating:** 1200; **Community Participation:** use of human resources in the community, interaction with community organizations; **Social Goal:** multicultural education; **School Goal:** multicultural education; **Primary Target:** all students; **Curricular Aims:** multicultural/social reconstructionist; **Instructional Aims:** human relations; **Classroom Environment:** multicultural/social reconstructionist; **School Practices:** transitional bilingual education, ESL, remedial classes, culturally diverse faculty, parental involvement in school policy decisions, culturally diverse staff, strong school-community public relations effort, inservice teacher training in multicultural education, Spanish as a second language, professionally staffed community relations office, bilingual curriculum, standard English as a second dialect, Asian language(s), ethnic studies curriculum; **Groups Studied:** African Americans, Arab Americans, Asian/Pacific Islander

Americans, French Americans, German Americans, Greek Americans, Hispanic (Latino/Chicano) Americans, Iranian Americans, Irish Americans, Italian Americans, Native Americans, Portuguese Americans, Scandinavian Americans, Slavic Americans; **Elements Studied:** attitudes, beliefs, body language, culture and personality, dialect, history, language, literature, music, physical characteristics, religion, social customs, social organization, social structure, values; **Participating Disciplines:** art, business, English, foreign languages, health, home economics, humanities, industrial arts, language arts, mathematics, music, physical education, reading, science, social studies, theater; **Locally Produced Materials:** yes; **Materials Available for Purchase:** *The Joint Activities, Multicultural Curriculum, Activities and Field Trip Guide.*

PATERSON CITY

Dr. Ruth L. Baskerville
Director, Instructional Services
660 14th Avenue
Paterson, NJ 07514
(201) 345-7112 ext. 110

Years In Operation: 11; **Grade Levels:** K-12; **Students Participating:** 24,000; **Community Participation:** community involvement in curriculum planning, use of community resources, interaction with community organizations; **Social Goal:** human relations; **School Goal:** multicultural/social reconstructionist; **Primary Target:** all students; **Curricular Aims:** multicultural/social reconstructionist; **Instructional Aims:** multicultural/social reconstructionist; **Classroom Environment:** multicultural/social reconstructionist; **School Practices:** transitional bilingual education, ESL, remedial classes, culturally diverse faculty, parental involvement in school policy decisions, human relations training for teachers, community involvement in school policy decisions, inservice teacher training in multicultural education, Spanish as a second language, bilingual curriculum, standard English as a second dialect, ethnic studies curriculum; **Groups Studied:** African Americans, Arab Americans, Asian/Pacific Islander Americans, Hispanic (Latino/Chicano) Americans, Irish Americans, Italian Americans, Native Americans, Bengali Americans; **Elements Studied:** art, attitudes, beliefs, foods, history, literature, music, religion, social customs; **Participating Disciplines:** art, English, foreign languages, humanities, language arts, music, reading, social studies, theater; **Locally Produced Materials:** yes;

TRENTON CITY

Everene D. Downing
Director/Curriculum Instruction, Staff Development
108 North Clinton Avenue
Trenton, NJ 08609
(609) 989-2897

Grade Levels: K-12; **Students Participating:** 12,665; **Community Participation:** community involvement in curriculum planning, use of community resources, use of human resources in the community, a community based instructional program, study of the community, interaction with community organizations; **Social Goal:** multicultural education; **School Goal:** multicultural/social reconstructionist; **Primary Target:** all students; **Curricular Aims:** multicultural/social reconstructionist; **Instructional Aims:** multicultural/social reconstructionist; **Classroom Environment:** multicultural/social reconstructionist; **School Practices:** transitional bilingual education, ESL, culturally diverse faculty, parental involvement in school policy decisions, culturally diverse staff, human relations training for teachers, community involvement in school policy decisions, strong school-community public relations effort, inservice teacher training in multicultural education, student involvement in curricular planning, Spanish as a second language, student involvement in school policy decisions, interracial student council, human relations training for students, bilingual curriculum, professionally staffed human relations team, student human relations council, bicultural curriculum, ethnic studies curriculum; **Groups Studied:** African Americans, Hispanic (Latino/Chicano) Americans, Italian Americans, Slavic Americans; **Elements Studied:** art, attitudes, beliefs, culture and personality, history, language, literature, material culture, music, social customs, social organization, social structure, values; **Participating Disciplines:** art, humanities, music, social studies, theater.

NEW MEXICO

ALBUQUERQUE

Wil Sandoval
Supervisor, Multicultural Education
3315 Louisiana NE
Albuquerque, NM 87125
(505) 883-0440

Years In Operation: 17; **Grade Levels:** K-12; **Students Participating:** 26,000; **Community Participation:** community involvement in curriculum planning, use of community resources, use of human resources in the community, interaction with community organizations; **Social Goal:** single-group studies, human relations; **School Goal:** multicultural education; **Primary Target:** all students; **Curricular Aims:** multicultural education; **Instructional Aims:** multicultural education; **Classroom Environment:** single-group studies, human relations; **School Practices:** transitional bilingual education, ESL, culturally diverse faculty, culturally diverse staff, community involvement in school policy decisions, strong school-community public relations effort, inservice teacher training in multicultural education, Spanish as a second language, bilingual curriculum, bicultural curriculum, ethnic studies curriculum; **Groups Studied:** African Americans, Asian/Pacific Islander Americans, Hispanic (Latino/Chicano) Americans, Native Americans; **Elements Studied:** art, attitudes, beliefs, dialect, foods, history, language, literature, music, social customs, social structure, values; **Participating Disciplines:** art, English, foreign languages, home economics, language arts, music, physical education, reading, social studies, theater; **Locally Produced Materials:** yes.

Gadsden Independent
Juan Sanchez
Director of Bilingual Education
P.O. Drawer 70
Anthony, NM 88021
(505) 882-6430

Years In Operation: 20; **Grade Levels:** K-12; **Students Participating:** 3,600; **Community Participation:** community involvement in curriculum planning, use of community resources, use of human resources in the community, interaction with community organizations; **Social Goal:** multicultural education; **School Goal:** multicultural/ social reconstructionist; **Primary Target:** minority students; **Curricular Aims:** multicultural education; **Instructional Aims:** multicultural education; **Classroom Environment:** multicultural education; **School Practices:** transitional bilingual education, ESL, remedial classes, culturally diverse faculty, parental involvement in school policy decisions, culturally diverse staff, inservice teacher training in multicultural education, student involvement in school policy decisions, interracial student council, bilingual curriculum, professionally staffed human relations team; **Locally Produced Materials:** yes.

Gallup-McKinley County
Esther V. Macias
Coordinator of Instruction
P.O. Box 1318
Gallup, NM 87305
(505) 722-7711

Grade Levels: K-12; **Students Participating:** 5,000; **Community Participation:** community involvement in curriculum planning; **Social Goal:** multicultural education; **School Goal:** teaching the culturally different; **Primary Target:** all students; **Curricular Aims:** multicultural education; **Instructional Aims:** multicultural education; **Classroom Environment:** single-group studies; **School Practices:** transitional bilingual education, ESL, bilingual curriculum, bicultural curriculum, multilingual curriculum, Native American language(s), ethnic studies curriculum; **Group Studied:** Native Americans; **Elements Studied:** art, history, kinship structure, literature, music, social customs, social organization, social structure, values; **Participating Disciplines:** art, English, foreign languages, humanities, language arts, music; **Locally Produced Materials:** yes.

Las Cruces
Mary Helen Garcia
505 South Main Street, Suite 249
Las Cruces, NM 88001
(505) 527-5800

Years In Operation: 2; **Grade Levels:** K-12; **Students Participating:** 1,870; **Social Goal:** single-group studies; **School Goal:** multicultural/social reconstructionist; **Primary Target:** minority students; **Curricular Aims:** teaching the culturally different; **Instructional Aims:** teaching the culturally different; **Classroom Environment:** multicultural/social reconstructionist; **School Practices:** transitional bilingual education, ESL, remedial classes, parental involvement in school policy decisions, culturally diverse staff, community involvement in school policy decisions, strong school-community public relations effort, inservice teacher training in multicultural education, Spanish as a second language, bilingual curriculum, bicultural curriculum, multilingual curriculum, ethnic studies curriculum; **Groups Studied:** Asian/Pacific Islander Americans, German Americans, Hispanic (Latino/Chicano) Americans; **Elements Studied:** foods, history, language, literature, material culture, music, social customs; **Participating Disciplines:** foreign languages, language arts, mathematics, music, reading, social studies; **Locally Produced Materials:** yes.

Roswell Independent
Monica Herrera
Director, Multicultural Education
200 West Chisum
Roswell, NM 88201
(505) 625-8100

Santa Fe
Esther Arredondo
Bilingual Education Coordinator
1300 Sierra Vista, Suite F
Santa Fe, NM 87505
(505) 989-5462

Years In Operation: 10; **Grade Levels:** 1-12; **Students Participating:** 2,100; **Community Participation:** community involvement in curriculum planning, use of community resources, use of human resources in the community, study of the community, interaction with community organizations; **Social Goal:** single-group studies; **School Goal:** multicultural education; **Primary Target:** all students; **Curricular Aims:** teaching the culturally different; **Instructional Aims:** teaching the culturally different; **Classroom Environment:** human relations; **School Practices:** transitional bilingual education, ESL, remedial classes, parental involvement in school policy decisions, culturally diverse staff, community involvement in school policy decisions, Spanish as a second language, interracial student council, human relations training for students, ethnic studies curriculum; **Elements Studied:** art, attitudes, beliefs, drama, foods, material culture, physical characteristics, religion, social customs; **Participating Disciplines:** art, foreign languages, language arts, mathematics, music, reading, theater.

NEW YORK

BUFFALO CITY
Samuel J. Alessi, Jr.
Assistant Superintendent
(716) 897-8131
Joanne Sadler
Supervisor of Curriculum Evaluation & Development
(716) 897-8129
229 Floss Avenue
Buffalo, NY 14215

NEW YORK CITY-CHANCELLOR'S OFFICE
Leslie Agard-Jones
Director, Office of Multicultural Education
131 Livingston Street, Room 621
Brooklyn, NY 11201
(718) 935-3984

SACHEM
Curriculum Director
245 Union Avenue
Holbrook, NY 11741
(516) 467-8202

Years In Operation: 30; **Grade Levels:** K-12; **Students Participating:** 14,000; **Community Participation:** use of community resources, use of human resources in the community, study of the community; **Social Goal:** teaching the culturally different; **School Goal:** teaching the culturally different; **Primary Target:** all students; **Curricular Aims:** multicultural education; **Instructional Aims:** multicultural education; **Classroom Environment:** multicultural/social reconstructionist; **School Practices:** ESL, remedial classes, culturally diverse faculty, parental involvement in school policy decisions, culturally diverse staff, human relations training for teachers, community involvement in school policy decisions, strong school-community public relations effort, student involvement in curriculum planning, Spanish as a second language, student involvement in school policy decisions, interracial student council, human relations training for students, professionally staffed community relations office, bicultural curriculum.

SYRACUSE CITY
Arcenia London
Staff Development Specialist
S.T.C. 501 Park Street
Syracuse, NY 13203
(315) 443-4808

Years In Operation: 5; **Grade Levels:** K-12; **Students Participating:** 22,680; **Community Participation:** community involvement in curriculum planning, use of community resources, use of human resources in the community, a community based instructional program, study of the community, interaction with community organizations; **Social Goal:** multicultural/social reconstructionist; **School Goal:** multicultural/ social reconstructionist; **Primary Target:** all students; **Curricular Aims:** multicultural/ social reconstructionist; **Instructional Aims:** multicultural/social reconstructionist; **Classroom Environment:** multicultural/social reconstructionist; **School Practices:** transitional bilingual education, ESL, remedial classes, human relations training for teachers, community involvement in school policy decisions, strong school-community public relations effort, inservice teacher training in multicultural education, student involvement in curriculum planning, Spanish as a second language, student involvement in school policy decisions, interracial student council, human relations training for students, professionally staffed community relations office, bilingual curriculum, professionally staffed human relations team, student human relations council, multilingual curriculum, ethnic studies curriculum; **Groups Studied:** African Americans, Asian/Pacific Islander Americans, Hispanic (Latino/Chicano) Americans, Native Americans, European Americans; **Elements Studied:** art, attitudes, beliefs, body language, culture and personality, dialect, drama, foods, history, kinship structure, language, literature, material culture, music, physical characteristics, religion, social customs, social organization, social structure, values; **Locally Produced Materials:** yes; **Materials Available for Purchase:** yes.

WAPPINGERS
Dr. Ann Marie Mullen
Assistant Superintendent for Instruction
Hollowbrook Park, Bldg. #3
15 Myers Corners Road
Wappingers Falls, NY 12590
(914) 298-5014
Lavinia Carter-Henry
Multicultural Education Consultant/Staff Specialist
Dutchess BOCES
350 Dutchess Turnpike
Poughkeepsie, NY 12603
(914) 486-4840

Years In Operation: 5; **Grade Levels:** K-12; **Students Participating:** 12,000; **Community Participation:** community involvement in curriculum planning, use of com-

munity resources, use of human resources in the community, interaction with community organizations; **Social Goal:** multicultural education; **School Goal:** multicultural education; **Primary Target:** all students; **Curricular Aims:** multicultural/social reconstructionist; **Instructional Aims:** multicultural/social reconstructionist; **Classroom Environment:** multicultural/social reconstructionist; **School Practices:** ESL, remedial classes, parental involvement in school policy decisions, human relations training for teachers, community involvement in school policy decisions, strong school-community public relations effort, inservice teacher training in multicultural education, Spanish as a second language, human relations training for students, Asian language(s), ethnic studies curriculum; **Elements Studied:** art, attitudes, beliefs, culture and personality, foods, history, kinship structure, language, literature, material culture, music, physical characteristics, religion, social customs, social organization, social structure, values.

Williamsville

Dr. Cindy Beeley
Instructional Specialist
415 Laurence Bell Drive
Williamsville, NY 14231-9070
(716) 626-8033

Years In Operation: 8; **Grade Levels:** K-12; **Students Participating:** 10,000; **Community Participation:** community involvement in curriculum planning, use of community resources, use of human resources in the community, interaction with community organizations, cultural diversity committee; **Social Goal:** single-group studies; **School Goal:** multicultural education; **Primary Target:** all students; **Curricular Aims:** multicultural education; **Instructional Aims:** multicultural/social reconstructionist; **Classroom Environment:** multicultural/social reconstructionist; **School Practices:** ESL, remedial classes, culturally diverse faculty, parental involvement in school policy decisions, culturally diverse staff, human relations training for teachers, community involvement in school policy decisions, strong school-community public relations effort, inservice teacher training in multicultural education, student involvement in curriculum planning, Spanish as a second language, student involvement in school policy decisions, interracial student council, human relations training for students, professionally staffed community relations office, Asian language(s); **Elements Studied:** art, attitudes, beliefs, culture and personality, drama, foods, history, language, literature, material culture, music, physical characteristics, religion, social customs, social organization, social structure, values; **Locally Produced Materials:** yes; **Materials Available for Purchase:** *Infusion of Multiculturalism in the Social Studies Curriculum* (four books: K-4, 5-6, 7-8, 9-12), *Cultural Diversity Resource Book.*

Yonkers City
Dr. Lois A. Jamieson
Assistant Superintendent
150 Rockland Avenue
Yonkers, NY 10705
(914) 376-8187

NORTH CAROLINA

Alamance County
Ted Henson
Director of Elementary Education
609 Ray Street
Graham, NC 27253
(910) 570-6647

Years In Operation: 12; **Grade Levels:** K-12; **Students Participating:** 11,000; **Community Participation:** use of community resources, use of human resources in the community, study of the community; **Social Goal:** human relations; **School Goal:** human relations; **Primary Target:** all students; **Curricular Aims:** teaching the culturally different; **Instructional Aims:** multicultural education; **Classroom Environment:** multicultural education; **School Practices:** ESL, remedial classes, culturally diverse faculty, parental involvement in school policy decisions, community involvement in school policy decisions, strong school-community public relations effort, professionally staffed community relations office.

Burke County
Dr. Richard Peck
Director of Student Services
P.O. Drawer 989
Morganton, NC 28680
(704) 439-4338

Years In Operation: 3; **Grade Levels:** K-12; **Students Participating:** 400; **Social Goal:** teaching the culturally different; **School Goal:** multicultural/social reconstructionist; **Primary Target:** minority students; **Curricular Aims:** teaching the culturally different; **Instructional Aims:** teaching the culturally different; **Classroom Environment:** single-group studies; **School Practices:** ESL, remedial classes, culturally diverse faculty, culturally diverse staff, community involvement in school policy decisions, strong school-community public relations effort, Spanish as a second language, interracial student council, human relations training for students, standard English as a second dialect.

Cabarrus County
Cathy Jewett
Curriculum Coordinator for Exceptional Children
P.O. Box 388
Concord, NC 28026
(704) 786-6191 ext. 148

Years In Operation: 3; **Grade Levels:** K-12; **Students Participating:** 15,000; **Community Participation:** community involvement in curriculum planning, use of community resources, use of human resources in the community, study of the community, interaction with community organizations; **Social Goal:** single-group studies; **School Goal:** multicultural education; **Primary Target:** all students; **Curricular Aims:** multicultural/social reconstructionist; **Instructional Aims:** multicultural/social reconstructionist; **Classroom Environment:** multicultural/social reconstructionist; **School Practices:** transitional bilingual education, ESL, remedial classes, culturally diverse faculty, parental involvement in school policy decisions, culturally diverse staff, human relations training for teachers, community involvement in school policy decisions, strong school-community public relations effort, inservice teacher training in multicultural education, student involvement in curriculum planning, Spanish as a second language, student involvement in school policy decisions, interracial student council, human relations training for students, bilingual curriculum, professionally staffed human relations team, student human relations council, multilingual curriculum, standard English as a second dialect, ethnic studies curriculum; **Elements Studied:** art, attitudes, beliefs, body language, culture and personality, dialect, foods, history, kinship structure, language, literature, material culture, music, religion, social customs, social organization, social structure, values; **Participating Disciplines:** English, foreign languages, home economics, humanities, industrial arts, language arts, mathematics, music, physical education, reading, science, social studies, theater.

Catawba County
Margaret Garrison
P.O. Box 1000
Newton, NC 28658
(704) 464-8333

Years In Operation: 9; **Grade Levels:** K-12; **Students Participating:** 12,865; **Community Participation:** use of community resources, use of human resources in the community, interaction with community organizations; **Social Goal:** single-group studies; **School Goal:** human relations; **Primary Target:** all students; **Curricular Aims:** human relations; **Instructional Aims:** multicultural education; **Classroom Environment:** multicultural/social reconstructionist; **School Practices:** ESL, culturally diverse faculty, parental involvement in school policy decisions, human relations training for teachers, community involvement in school policy decisions, strong school-community public relations effort, inservice teacher training in multicultural education, Spanish as a second language, human relations training for students, professionally staffed human relations team.

CRAVEN COUNTY
Terrence Hicks
Director of Students Services
3000 Trent Road
New Bern, NC 28561
(919) 514-6341

Years In Operation: 1; **Grade Levels:** 6-9; **Students Participating:** 3,486; **Social Goal:** multicultural education; **School Goal:** human relations; **Primary Target:** all students; **Curricular Aims:** multicultural education; **Instructional Aims:** multicultural/social reconstructionist; **Classroom Environment:** multicultural/social reconstructionist; **School Practices:** human relations training for teachers, inservice teacher training in multicultural education, ethnic studies curriculum; **Groups Studied:** African Americans, Hispanic (Latino/Chicano) Americans, Native Americans; **Elements Studied:** attitudes, beliefs, history, social customs, social structure; **Participating Disciplines:** English, language arts, social studies.

FORSYTH COUNTY
Pamela S. Frazier
African-American Curriculum Project Facilitator
1605 Miller Street
Winston Salem, NC 27102-2513
(910) 727-2372

GASTON COUNTY
Ann Neal
Technical Assistant for Elementary Education
P.O. Box 1397
Gastonia, NC 28053
(704) 866-6100

Years In Operation: 3; **Grade Levels:** K-12; **Students Participating:** 275; **Social Goal:** teaching the culturally different; **School Goal:** teaching the culturally different; **Primary Target:** minority students; **Curricular Aims:** teaching the culturally different; **Instructional Aims:** teaching the culturally different; **Classroom Environment:** teaching the culturally different; **School Practices:** ESL, culturally diverse faculty, inservice teacher training in multicultural education, standard English as a second dialect; **Elements Studied:** body language, culture and personality, literature, material culture; **Participating Disciplines:** English, language arts, reading.

Mecklenburg County
Anne Udall
Coordinating Director of Curriculum
Stonewall Plaza, Suite 506
Charlotte, NC 28202
(704) 343-6955

Nash County
Lee Grier
Director of Staff Development
930 Eastern Avenue
Nashville, NC 27856
(919) 459-5232

Years In Operation: 3; **Grade Levels:** 1-12; **Community Participation:** use of community resources, use of human resources in the community, interaction with community organizations; **Social Goal:** multicultural education; **School Goal:** multicultural education; **Primary Target:** all students; **Curricular Aims:** human relations; **Instructional Aims:** multicultural education; **Classroom Environment:** multicultural/social reconstructionist; **School Practices:** ESL, culturally diverse faculty, parental involvement in school policy decisions, human relations training for teachers, community involvement in school policy decisions, strong school-community public relations effort, inservice teacher training in multicultural education, Spanish as a second language, interracial student council, human relations training for students, professionally staffed community relations office, Asian language(s).

New Hanover County
Cynthia Henry
Social Studies/Foreign Language Supervisor
1802 South 15th Street
Wilmington, NC 28401
(910) 763-5431

Years In Operation: 4; **Grade Levels:** K-12; **Students Participating:** 20,000; **Community Participation:** community involvement in curriculum planning, use of community resources, use of human resources in the community, study of the community, interaction with community organizations; **Social Goal:** human relations; **School Goal:** teaching the culturally different; **Primary Target:** all students; **Curricular Aims:** multicultural education; **Instructional Aims:** multicultural education; **Classroom Environment:** single-group studies; **School Practices:** ESL, remedial classes, culturally diverse faculty, parental involvement in school policy decisions, culturally diverse staff, human relations training for teachers, community involvement in school policy decisions, strong school-community public relations effort, inservice teacher training in multicultural education, student involvement in curricular planning, student involvement in school policy decisions, interracial student council, human relations training for students; **Elements Studied:** art, attitudes, beliefs, culture and personality, drama, foods, history, literature, music, religion, social customs, values; **Participating Discipline:** social studies; **Locally Produced Materials:** yes.

RANDOLPH COUNTY
Ruth Spargo
Limited-English Proficiency Program
2222-C South Fayetteville Street
Asheboro, NC 27203
(910) 318-6059

Years In Operation: 5; **Grade Levels:** K-12; **Students Participating:** 275; **Community Participation:** parent advisory council; **Social Goal:** teaching the culturally different; **School Goal:** teaching the culturally different; **Primary Target:** minority students; **Curricular Aims:** teaching the culturally different; **Instructional Aims:** teaching the culturally different; **Classroom Environment:** single-group studies; **School Practices:** ESL, remedial classes, culturally diverse faculty, parental involvement in school policy decisions, strong school-community public relations effort, inservice teacher training in multicultural education, Spanish as a second language, human relations training for students.

UNION COUNTY
Gail Latham
Director of Secondary Education
500 North Main St., Suite 700
Monroe, NC 28110
(704) 283-3651

Grade Levels: K-12; **Students Participating:** 17,000; **Community Participation:** community involvement in curriculum planning, use of community resources, use of human resources in the community, a community based instructional program, study of the community, interaction with community organizations; **Social Goal:** multicultural education; **School Goal:** multicultural education; **Primary Target:** all students; **Curricular Aims:** multicultural education; **Instructional Aims:** multicultural education; **Classroom Environment:** multicultural/social reconstructionist; **School Practices:** ESL, remedial classes, culturally diverse faculty, parental involvement in school policy decisions, culturally diverse staff, human relations training for teachers, community involvement in school policy decisions, strong school-community public relations effort, inservice teacher training in multicultural education, Spanish as a second language, interracial student council, human relations training for students, standard English as a second dialect.

NORTH DAKOTA

Bismark

Dr. Sharon Johnson
Superintendent
400 Avenue E East
Bismark, ND 58501
(701) 221-3706

Years In Operation: 7; **Grade Levels:** K-6; **Students Participating:** 6,000; **Community Participation:** use of community resources, use of human resources in the community, interaction with community organizations; **Social Goal:** multicultural education; **School Goal:** human relations; **Primary Target:** minority students; **Curricular Aims:** multicultural education; **Instructional Aims:** multicultural education; **Classroom Environment:** multicultural/social reconstructionist; **School Practices:** transitional bilingual education, ESL, remedial classes, school involved in community action projects, community involvement in school policy decisions, strong school-community public relations effort, inservice teacher training in multicultural education, professionally staffed community relations office, multilingual curriculum, standard English as a second dialect, Native American Language(s); **Group Studied:** Native Americans; **Elements Studied:** art, attitudes, beliefs, culture and personality, social customs, social organizaion; **Locally Produced Materials:** yes.

Fargo

Dr. Glenn Melney
Assistant Superintendent, FPS
1104 2nd Avenue South
Fargo, ND 58103
(701) 241-4831

Years In Operation: 20; **Grade Levels:** K-12; **Students Participating:** 502; **Community Participation:** community involvement in curriculum planning, use of community resources, use of human resources in the community, a community based instructional program, study of the community, interaction with community organizations; **Social Goal:** teaching the culturally different; **School Goal:** human relations; **Primary Target:** all students; **Curricular Aims:** teaching the culturally different; **Instructional Aims:** multicultural education; **Classroom Environment:** multicultural/social reconstructionist; **School Practices:** transitional bilingual education, ESL, human relations training for teachers, community involvement in school policy decisions, strong school-community public relations effort, inservice teacher training in multicultural education, student involvement in curriculum planning, Spanish as a second language, student involvement in school policy decisions, human relations training for students, bilingual curriculum, standard English as a second dialect, ethnic studies curriculum; **Group Studied:** Native Americans; **Elements Studied:** art, attitudes, beliefs, culture and personality, social customs, social organizaion; **Participating Disciplines:** art, social studies; **Locally Produced Materials:** yes.

OHIO

AKRON CITY
Beradine Burchett
Learning Specialist
65 Steiner Avenue
Akron, OH 44301
(216) 434-1661 ext. 3205

Years In Operation: 7; **Grade Levels:** 9; **Students Participating:** 200; **Community Participation:** community involvement in curriculum planning, use of community resources, use of human resources in the community; **Social Goal:** human relations; **School Goal:** teaching the culturally different; **Primary Target:** all students; **Curricular Aims:** multicultural education; **Instructional Aims:** multicultural/social reconstructionist; **Classroom Environment:** multicultural/social reconstructionist; **School Practices:** transitional bilingual education, culturally diverse faculty, parental involvement in school policy decisions, culturally diverse staff, human relations training for teachers, community involvement in school policy decisions, inservice teacher training in multicultural education, bilingual curriculum, ethnic studies curriculum; **Group Studied:** African Americans; **Elements Studied:** art, culture and personality, drama, foods, history, literature, music, social customs; **Participating Disciplines:** art, foreign languages, language arts, music, reading, social studies; **Locally Produced Materials:** yes.

CINCINNATI CITY
Kathleen T. Ware
Director, Quality Improvement
230 East Ninth Street
Cincinnati, OH 45202
(513) 369-4802

Years In Operation: 5; **Grade Levels:** K-12; **Students Participating:** 50,000; **Community Participation:** community involvement in curriculum planning; **Social Goal:** multicultural education; **School Goal:** multicultural education; **Primary Target:** all students; **Curricular Aims:** multicultural education; **Instructional Aims:** multicultural education; **Classroom Environment:** multicultural education; **School Practices:** culturally diverse faculty, parental involvement in school policy decisions, interracial student council, ethnic studies curriculum; **Groups Studied:** African Americans, Appalachian Americans; **Elements Studied:** dialect, drama, history, literature, music; **Participating Disciplines:** art, English, language arts, mathematics, music, science, social studies.

Cleveland City
Mayethel V. White
Director, General Education
1380 East Sixth Street
Cleveland, OH 44114
(216) 574-8667

Years In Operation: 10; **Grade Levels:** K-12; **Students Participating:** 70,933; **Community Participation:** community involvement in curriculum planning; **Social Goal:** single-group studies; **School Goal:** teaching the culturally different; **Primary Target:** all students; **Curricular Aims:** teaching the culturally different; **Instructional Aims:** multicultural education; **Classroom Environment:** single-group studies; **School Practices:** transitional bilingual education, ESL, culturally diverse faculty, human relations training for teachers, community involvement in school policy decisions, inservice teacher training in multicultural education, student involvement in curricular planning, student involvement in school policy decisions, interracial student council, human relations training for students, professionally staffed community relations office, professionally staffed human relations team, bicultural curriculum; **Locally Produced Materials:** yes.

Columbus City
Josephine Scott
Supervisor, Multicultural Education Office
Northgate Center
6655 Sharon Woods Boulevard
Columbus, OH 43229
(614) 365-5039

Years In Operation: 5; **Grade Levels:** K-12; **Community Participation:** use of community resources, use of human resources in the community, study of the community, interaction with community organizations, local business support of multicultural programs; **Social Goal:** multicultural education; **School Goal:** multicultural education; **Primary Target:** all students; **Curricular Aims:** multicultural/social reconstructionist; **Instructional Aims:** multicultural/social reconstructionist; **Classroom Environment:** multicultural/social reconstructionist; **School Practices:** culturally diverse faculty, parental involvement in school policy decisions, human relations training for teachers, inservice teacher training in multicultural education, interracial student council; **Elements Studied:** art, attitudes, beliefs, body language, culture and personality, dialect, foods, history, language, literature, music, social customs, social organization, social structure, values; **Participating Disciplines:** art, business, English, foreign languages, health, home economics, humanities, industrial arts, language arts, mathematics, music, physical education, reading, science, social studies, theater; **Locally Produced Materials:** yes.

Dayton City
Bickley Lucas
Executive Director, Academic Services
2013 West Third Street
Dayton, OH 45417
(513) 262-2767

Years In Operation: 1; **Grade Levels:** K-12; **Students Participating:** 28,000; **Community Participation:** community involvement in curriculum planning, use of community resources, use of human resources in the community, interaction with community organizations, community task force; **Social Goal:** human relations; **School Goal:** human relations; **Primary Target:** all students; **Curricular Aims:** multicultural education; **Instructional Aims:** multicultural education; **Classroom Environment:** multicultural/social reconstructionist; **School Practices:** ESL, remedial classes, culturally diverse faculty, parental involvement in school policy decisions, culturally diverse staff, human relations training for teachers, community involvement in school policy decisions, strong school-community public relations effort, inservice teacher training in multicultural education, student involvement in curricular planning, student involvement in school policy decisions, interracial student council, human relations training for students, bilingual curriculum, professionally staffed human relations team, student human relations council, standard English as a second dialect, Asian language(s), ethnic studies curriculum; **Groups Studied:** African Americans, Arab Americans, Asian/Pacific Islander Americans, Hispanic (Latino/Chicano) Americans, Iranian Americans, Native Americans; **Elements Studied:** art, attitudes, beliefs, body language, culture and personality, dialect, drama, foods, history, kinship structure, language, literature, material culture, music, religion, social customs, social organization, social structure, values; **Participating Disciplines:** art, English, foreign languages, health, home economics, humanities, language arts, mathematics, music, physical education, reading, science, social studies, theater.

Lakota
Janet Gorman
Director, Elementary Curriculum
Rick Bateman
Director, Secondary Curriculum
5030 Tylersville Road
West Chester, OH 45069
(513) 874-5505

Years In Operation: 2; **Grade Levels:** 9-12; **Community Participation:** community involvement in curriculum planning, use of community resources, use of human resources in the community, interaction with community organizations; **Social Goal:** human relations; **School Goal:** human relations; **Primary Target:** all students; **Curricular Aims:** multicultural/social reconstructionist; **Instructional Aims:** multicultural education; **Classroom Environment:** multicultural education; **School Practices:** ESL, remedial classes, parental involvement in school policy decisions, human relations training for teachers, strong school-community public relations effort, inservice teacher training in multicultural education, student involvement in school policy decisions; **Elements Studied:** art, history, literature, music, religion, values.

Northwest
Frank Margello
Principal, Northwest High School
10761 Pippin Road
Cincinnati, OH 45231
(513) 742-6340

Years In Operation: 3; **Grade Levels:** 9-12; **Students Participating:** 40; **Community Participation:** use of community resources, use of human resources in the community, interaction with community organizations; **Social Goal:** multicultural education; **School Goal:** multicultural education; **Primary Target:** all students; **Curricular Aims:** multicultural education; **Instructional Aims:** multicultural/social reconstructionist; **Classroom Environment:** multicultural/social reconstructionist; **School Practices:** culturally diverse faculty, parental involvement in school policy decisions, community involvement in school policy decisions, strong school-community public relations effort, student involvement in school policy decisions, interracial student council; **Elements Studied:** culture and personality, foods, history, literature, material culture, music, physical characteristics, social customs.

Springfield City
Jeannine Fox
49 East College Avenue
Springfield, OH 45504
(513) 328-2000

Years In Operation: 1; **Grade Levels:** K-12; **Students Participating:** 11,500; **Community Participation:** community involvement in curriculum planning, use of community resources, use of human resources in the community, study of the community, interaction with community organizations; **Social Goal:** multicultural education; **School Goal:** multicultural education; **Primary Target:** all students; **Curricular Aims:** multicultural/social reconstructionist; **Instructional Aims:** multicultural education; **Classroom Environment:** multicultural/social reconstructionist; **School Practices:** ESL, culturally diverse faculty, parental involvement in school policy decisions, culturally diverse staff, human relations training for teachers, community involvement in school policy decisions, strong school-community public relations effort, inservice teacher training in multicultural education, Spanish as a second language, interracial student council, human relations training for students, professionally staffed community relations office, ethnic studies curriculum; **Groups Studied:** African Americans, Arab Americans, Asian/Pacific Islander Americans, French Americans, German Americans, Greek Americans, Hispanic (Latino/Chicano) Americans, Irish Americans, Italian Americans, Native Americans; **Elements Studied:** art, attitudes, beliefs, culture and personality, dialect, drama, foods, history, kinship structure, language, literature, material culture, music, physical characteristics, religion, social customs, social organization, social structure, values; **Participating Disciplines:** art, English, foreign languages, health, home economics, language arts, mathematics, music, physical education, reading, science, social studies, theater.

TOLEDO CITY
Richard Brunt
420 East Manhattan
Toledo, OH 43608
(419) 729-8200

Years In Operation: 3; **Grade Levels:** 1-6; **Students Participating:** 10,000; **Social Goal:** multicultural education; **School Goal:** human relations; **Primary Target:** all students; **Curricular Aims:** human relations; **Instructional Aims:** multicultural education; **Classroom Environment:** single-group studies; **School Practices:** inservice teacher training in multicultural education, interracial student council, human relations training for students, professionally staffed human relations team, student human relations council; **Elements Studied:** art, foods, history, literature, material culture, music, physical characteristics, religion.

WORTHINGTON CITY
P.R. West
Multicultural Coordinator
752 High Street
Worthington, OH 43085
(614) 431-6500

Years In Operation: 3; **Grade Levels:** K-12; **Students Participating:** 11,000; **Community Participation:** use of community resources, use of human resources in the community, a community based instructional program; **Social Goal:** multicultural education; **School Goal:** multicultural education; **Primary Target:** all students; **Curricular Aims:** single-group studies; **Instructional Aims:** multicultural education; **Classroom Environment:** multicultural/social reconstructionist; **School Practices:** ESL, human relations training for teachers, inservice teacher training in multicultural education, interracial student council, human relations training for students, multilingual curriculum, Asian language(s), ethnic studies curriculum; **Groups Studied:** African Americans, Native Americans; **Elements Studied:** art, attitudes, beliefs, culture and personality, history, literature, religion, social customs, social organization, social structure, values; **Participating Disciplines:** art, English, social studies;**Locally Produced Materials:** yes; **Materials Available for Purchase:** *The Contributions of African American Scientists and Inventors to Our Country and the World: Past and Present & Diversity: Why It's Important to Me—The Collective Visions of Worthington Students*, edited by P.R. West ($5.00).

OKLAHOMA

Edmond
Dr. Brenda Lyons
Assistant Superintendent
1001 West Danforth
Edmond, OK 73003
(405) 340-2207

Years In Operation: 21; **Grade Levels:** K-12; **Students Participating:** 600; **Community Participation:** community involvement in curriculum planning, use of community resources, use of human resources in the community, interaction with community organizations; **Social Goal:** single-group studies; **School Goal:** human relations; **Primary Target:** minority students; **Curricular Aims:** single-group studies; **Instructional Aims:** teaching the culturally different; **Classroom Environment:** multicultural/ social reconstructionist; **School Practices:** remedial classes, culturally diverse faculty, parental involvement in school policy decisions, culturally diverse staff, inservice teacher training in multicultural education, student involvement in curricular planning, multilingual curriculum, ethnic studies curriculum; **Group Studied:** Native Americans; **Elements Studied:** art, attitudes, beliefs, culture and personality, foods, history, kinship structure, language, material culture, music, social customs, social organization, social structure, values; **Participating Disciplines:** art, English, foreign languages, home economics, language arts, mathematics, music, reading, science, social studies.

Moore
Wilmer Cooper
Human Relations Coordinator
Westmoore High School
12613 South Western
Oklahoma City, OK 73170
(405) 692-5724
Carole Dixon
Human Relations Coordinator
Moore High School
300 North Eastern
Moore, OK 73160
(405) 793-3100

Years In Operation: 3; **Grade Levels:** K-12; **Students Participating:** 10,000; **Social Goal:** human relations; **School Goal:** multicultural education; **Primary Target:** all students; **Curricular Aims:** teaching the culturally different; **Instructional Aims:** teaching the culturally different; **Classroom Environment:** single-group studies; **School Practices:** ESL, remedial classes, culturally diverse faculty, culturally diverse staff, human relations training for teachers, community involvement in school policy decisions, strong school-community public relations effort, inservice teacher training in multicultural education, student involvement in curriculum planning, student involvement in school policy decisions; **Locally Produced Materials:** yes.

MIDWEST CITY
Bill Sutton
Social Studies Coordinator
7217 SE 15th Street
Midwest City, OK 73110
(405) 737-4461 ext. 263

OKLAHOMA CITY
Dr. Hawthorn Faison
Director of Curriculum
3416 NW 17
Oklahoma City, OK 73107
(405) 297-6497

Years In Operation: 6; **Grade Levels:** K-5; **Students Participating:** 1,436; **Community Participation:** community involvement in curriculum planning, use of community resources, use of human resources in the community, study of the community, interaction with community organizations; **Social Goal:** human relations; **School Goal:** human relations; **Primary Target:** all students; **Curricular Aims:** human relations; **Instructional Aims:** multicultural education; **Classroom Environment:** multicultural/social reconstructionist; **School Practices:** transitional bilingual education, ESL, remedial classes, culturally diverse faculty, parental involvement in school policy decisions, culturally diverse staff, human relations training for teachers, community involvement in school policy decisions, inservice teacher training in multicultural education, Spanish as a second language, student involvement in school policy decisions, interracial student council, bilingual curriculum, bicultural curriculum, ethnic studies curriculum; **Groups Studied:** African Americans, Asian/Pacific Islander Americans, Hispanic (Latino/Chicano) Americans, Native Americans; **Elements Studied:** art, beliefs, body language, culture and personality, dialect, drama, foods, history, kinship structure, language, literature, material culture, music, physical characteristics, religion, social customs, values; **Participating Disciplines:** art, English, language arts, mathematics, music, physical education, reading, science, social studies; **Locally Produced Materials:** yes.

Putnam
Cleda Spaeth
Staff Development Coordinator
5401 NW 40th
Oklahoma City, OK 73122
(405) 495-5200 ext. 217

Years In Operation: 4; **Grade Levels:** K-3,7; **Students Participating:** 3,500; **Community Participation:** community involvement in curriculum planning, use of community resources, use of human resources in the community, interaction with community organizations; **Social Goal:** single-group studies; **School Goal:** teaching the culturally different; **Primary Target:** all students; **Curricular Aims:** multicultural education; **Instructional Aims:** multicultural education; **Classroom Environment:** multicultural/social reconstructionist; **School Practices:** transitional bilingual education, ESL, culturally diverse faculty, human relations training for teachers, inservice teacher training in multicultural education, Spanish as a second language, bilingual curriculum, bicultural curriculum, multilingual curriculum, standard English as a second dialect; **Elements Studied:** art, culture and personality, foods, language, literature, material culture, music, social customs; **Participating Disciplines:** art, foreign languages, reading, social studies; **Locally Produced Materials:** yes.

Tulsa
Ron Foore, Ph.D.
Coordinator, Social Studies
2525 South 101 East Avenue
Tulsa, OK 74129
(918) 621-6800

Years In Operation: 5; **Grade Levels:** K-12; **Students Participating:** 42,000; **Community Participation:** community involvement in curriculum planning, use of community resources, use of human resources in the community, a community based instructional program, study of the community, interaction with community organizations; **Social Goal:** single-group studies; **School Goal:** human relations; **Primary Target:** all students; **Curricular Aims:** single-group studies; **Instructional Aims:** multicultural education; **Classroom Environment:** single-group studies; **School Practices:** transitional bilingual education, ESL, remedial classes, culturally diverse faculty, parental involvement in school policy decisions, culturally diverse staff, human relations training for teachers, community involvement in school policy decisions, strong school-community public relations effort, inservice teacher training in multicultural education, Spanish as a second language, student involvement in school policy decisions, interracial student council, human relations training for students, professionally staffed community relations office, bilingual curriculum, professionally staffed human relations team, Asian language(s), Native American language(s), ethnic studies curriculum; **Groups Studied:** African Americans, Arab Americans, Asian/Pacific Islander Americans, Hispanic (Latino/Chicano) Americans, Native Americans; **Elements Studied:** art, attitudes, beliefs, body language, culture and personality, dialect, drama, foods, history, kinship structure, language, literature, material culture, music, physical characteristics, religion, social customs, social organization, social structure, values; **Participating Disciplines:** art, business, English, foreign languages, health, home economics, humanities, industrial arts, language arts, mathematics, music, physical education, reading, science, social studies, theater; **Locally Produced Materials:** yes.

UNION
Helen Elliott
Principal, Sixth Grade Center
10100 East 61st Street
Tulsa, OK 74134
(918) 459-2730

OREGON

BEND/LAPINE
Diane Hensley
Director of Special Education
520 NW Wall Street
Bend, OR 97701
(503) 383-6050

Years In Operation: 8; **Grade Levels:** K-12; **Students Participating:** 45; **Community Participation:** use of human resources in the community; **Social Goal:** teaching the culturally different; **School Goal:** human relations; **Primary Target:** minority students; **Curricular Aims:** teaching the culturally different; **Instructional Aims:** multicultural education; **School Practices:** ESL, standard English as a second dialect.

EUGENE
Bettie Sing Luke
Multicultural Trainer/Equity Specialist
200 North Monroe
Eugene, OR 97402
(503) 687-3464

NORTH CLACKAMAS
Terri Pavlonnis
Director of Instructional Services
4444 SE Lake Road
Milwaukie, OR 97222
(503) 653-3612

Years In Operation: 1; **Grade Levels:** 9-12; **Community Participation:** community involvement in curriculum planning, use of community resources, use of human resources in the community, interaction with community organizations.

PORTLAND
Carolyn Leonard
Multiethnic Coordinator
501 North Dixon Street
Portland, OR 97227
(503) 331-3383

Years In Operation: 10; **Grade Levels:** K-12; **Students Participating:** 54,496; **Community Participation:** community involvement in curriculum planning, use of community resources, use of human resources in the community, interaction with community organizations; **Social Goal:** multicultural education; **School Goal:** teaching the culturally different; **Primary Target:** all students; **Curricular Aims:** multicultural education; **Instructional Aims:** multicultural education; **Classroom Environment:** multicultural education; **School Practices:** parental involvement in school policy decisions, community involvement in school policy decisions, inservice teacher training in multicultural education, ethnic studies curriculum; **Groups Studied:** African Americans, Arab Americans, Asian/Pacific Islander Americans, Hispanic (Latino/Chicano) Americans, Native Americans; **Elements Studied:** art, attitudes, beliefs, history, literature, music; **Participating Disciplines:** art, business, English, foreign languages, health, home economics, humanities, industrial arts, language arts, mathematics, music, physical education, reading, science, social studies, theater; **Locally Produced Materials:** yes; **Materials Available for Purchase:**

99-0146A	African American Baseline Essays (Includes 99-0148) under revision	$25.00
99-0147	African American Lesson Plans K-5, Nov. 1988	$35.00
99-0148	Using the African American Baseline Essays, 1989	$0.25
99-0150	Hispanic Heritage Lesson Plans K-12, Sept. 1989 (Includes 99-0151, 99-0152, 99-0153, 99-0154, 99-0155, 99-0156)	$30.00
99-0151	Grades K-2	$5.00
99-0152	Grades 3-5	$5.00
99-0153	Grade 6 Unit Plan	$5.00
99-0154	Grades 6-8	$5.00
99-0155	Grades 9-12	$5.00
99-0156	Hispanic American Profiles/Posters	$6.00

99-0157	Multicultural/Multiethnic Education in Portland Public Schools, 1988	$1.50
99-0264	Hispanic Heritage Baseline Essays	NPA
99-0265	American Indian Baseline Essays	NPA
99-0304	African Chants and Songs (Teacher's Resource Book and Tape)	$10.00

Make payable to Portland Public Schools. Prices include shipping by USPS Library Rate. The cost of publications are subject to revision. Orders should be sent to: Craig Kurath, Curriculum and Instruction Support Services, PO Box 3107, Portland, OR, 97208.

Salem/Keizer
Marsha Benjamin Moyer
Administrator, Multicultural Education
1340 State Street, SE
Salem, OR 97301
(503) 399-3075

Springfield
Rita Webber
Social Studies Specialist
525 Mill Street
Springfield, OR 97477
(541) 726-3213

PENNSYLVANIA

Allentown
Myron Yoder
Social Studies Curriculum Coordinator
31 South Penn Street, P.O. Box 328
Allentown, PA 18105
(610) 821-2615

Bethlehem
Michele Kostem
Assistant Superintendent
1516 Sycamore Street
Bethlehem, PA 18017
(610) 861-0500

Years In Operation: 20; **Grade Levels:** K-12; **Students Participating:** 9,000; **Community Participation:** community involvement in curriculum planning, use of com-

munity resources, use of human resources in the community, a community based instructional program, interaction with community organizations; **Social Goal:** multicultural education; **School Goal:** multicultural education; **Primary Target:** all students; **Curricular Aims:** human relations; **Instructional Aims:** multicultural education; **Classroom Environment:** multicultural education; **School Practices:** ESL, culturally diverse faculty, parental involvement in school policy decisions, culturally diverse staff, community involvement in school policy decisions, strong school-community public relations effort, inservice teacher training in multicultural education, student involvement in curricular planning, student involvement in school policy decisions, interracial student council, professionally staffed community relations office, professionally staffed human relations team, standard English as a second dialect; **Elements Studied:** foods, language, music, religion, social customs; **Participating Disciplines:** language arts, social studies.

NORTH PENN

Sandra D. Mangano, Ed.D.
Supervisor, K-1 Multicultural Curriculum & Staff Development
401 East Hancock Street
Lansdale, PA 19446
(215) 368-0400 ext. 269

Years In Operation: 4; **Grade Levels:** K-12; **Students Participating:** 11,000; **Community Participation:** community involvement in curriculum planning, use of community resources, study of the community, interaction with community organizations; **Social Goal:** human relations; **School Goal:** human relations; **Primary Target:** all students; **Curricular Aims:** multicultural/social reconstructionist; **Instructional Aims:** multicultural education; **Classroom Environment:** multicultural education; **School Practices:** ESL, culturally diverse faculty, parental involvement in school policy decisions, culturally diverse staff, human relations training for teachers, community involvement in school policy decisions, strong school-community public relations effort, inservice teacher training in multicultural education, interracial student council, human relations training for students, professionally staffed community relations office.

PHILADELPHIA CITY

Deborah Wei
Multicultural Studies—Office of Curriculum Support
21st & Parkway
Philadelphia, PA 19103
(215) 299-8912

Years In Operation: 21; **Grade Levels:** K-12; **Students Participating:** 201,496; **Community Participation:** community involvement in curriculum planning, use of community resources, use of human resources in the community, a community based instructional program, study of the community, interaction with community organiza-

tions; **Social Goal:** multicultural/social reconstructionist; **School Goal:** multicultural/social reconstructionist; **Primary Target:** all students; **Curricular Aims:** multicultural/social reconstructionist; **Instructional Aims:** multicultural/social reconstructionist; **Classroom Environment:** multicultural/social reconstructionist; **School Practices:** transitional bilingual education, ESL, remedial classes, culturally diverse faculty, parental involvement in school policy decisions, culturally diverse staff, human relations training for teachers, community involvement in school policy decisions, strong school-community public relations effort, inservice teacher training in multicultural education, student involvement in curricular planning, Spanish as a second language, student involvement in school policy decisions, interracial student council, human relations training for students, professionally staffed community relations office, bilingual curriculum, professionally staffed human relations team, student human relations council, bicultural curriculum, multilingual curriculum, Asian language(s), ethnic studies curriculum; **Groups Studied:** African Americans, Asian/Pacific Islander Americans, Hispanic (Latino/Chicano) Americans; **Elements Studied:** art, attitudes, beliefs, culture and personality, drama, history, kinship structure, language, literature, material culture, religion, social customs, social organization, social structure, values; **Participating Disciplines:** art, English, foreign languages, humanities, language arts, social studies; **Locally Produced Materials:** yes; **Materials Available for Purchase:** yes.

PITTSBURGH

Dr. Stanley Denton
School Support Specialist for Multicultural Education
Connelley Administrative Center
1601 Bedford Avenue
Pittsburgh, PA 15219
(412) 338-8031

READING

Dr. Marcia Glon-Alvarado
Director of Bilingual Education
800 Washington Street
Reading, PA 19601-3691
(610) 371-5665

West Chester
Dr. Janet P. Shaner
Assistant to the Superintendent
829 Paoli Pike
West Chester, PA 19380
(610) 436-7117

Years In Operation: 1; **Grade Levels:** K-12; **Community Participation:** community involvement in curriculum planning, use of human resources in the community; **Social Goal:** single-group studies; **School Goal:** human relations; **Primary Target:** all students; **Curricular Aims:** multicultural/social reconstructionist; **Instructional Aims:** multicultural education; **Classroom Environment:** single-group studies; **School Practices:** human relations training for teachers, inservice teacher training in multicultural education, student involvement in curricular planning, Spanish as a second language, ethnic studies curriculum; **Groups Studied:** African Americans, Asian/Pacific Islander Americans, Hispanic (Latino/Chicano) Americans, Native Americans; **Elements Studied:** art, literature, music, religion, social customs; **Participating Disciplines:** art, business, English, foreign languages, health, home economics, industrial arts, language arts, mathematics, music, physical education, reading, science, social studies.

SOUTH CAROLINA

Aiken County
Dr. Alice Sheehan
Director of Staff Development
P.O. Box 1137
Aiken, SC 29801
(803) 641-2490

Grade Levels: K-12; **Community Participation:** use of human resources in the community; **Social Goal:** human relations; **School Goal:** human relations; **Primary Target:** all students; **Curricular Aims:** multicultural/social reconstructionist; **Instructional Aims:** multicultural/social reconstructionist; **Classroom Environment:** multicultural/social reconstructionist; **School Practices:** ESL, remedial classes, culturally diverse faculty, parental involvement in school policy decisions, human relations training for teachers, inservice teacher training in multicultural education; **Elements Studied:** art, attitudes, beliefs, body language, culture and personality, dialect, drama, foods, history, language, literature, material culture, music, physical characteristics, religion, social customs, social organization.

CHARLESTON COUNTY
Bill Smyth
Supervisor, Social Studies
75 Calhoun Street
Charleston, SC 29401
(803) 937-6484

Years In Operation: 3; **Grade Levels:** K-12; **Students Participating:** 46,000; **Community Participation:** community involvement in curriculum planning, use of community resources, use of human resources in the community, interaction with community organizations; **Social Goal:** human relations; **School Goal:** human relations; **Primary Target:** all students; **Curricular Aims:** human relations; **Instructional Aims:** multicultural education; **Classroom Environment:** multicultural education; **School Practices:** ESL, remedial classes, culturally diverse faculty, parental involvement in school policy decisions, culturally diverse staff, human relations training for teachers, community involvement in school policy decisions, strong school-community public relations effort, inservice teacher training in multicultural education, Spanish as a second language, student involvement in school policy decisions, interracial student council, human relations training for students, a professionally staffed community relations office.

DARLINGTON COUNTY
Valerie Harrison
Assistant Superintendent for Curriculum & Instruction
102 Park Street
Darlington, SC 29532
(803) 398-5100

HORRY COUNTY
Ginny Kintz
Specialist for Multicultural Affairs
1605 Horry Street
Conway, SC 29527
(803) 248-8620
Susan Hughes
Assistant Principal
Conway High School
2201 Church Street
Conway, SC 29526
(803) 248-6321

Years In Operation: 2; **Grade Levels:** K-12; **Students Participating:** 25,700; **Community Participation:** community involvement in curriculum planning, use of community resources, use of human resources in the community, interaction with community organizations; **Social Goal:** human relations; **School Goal:** multicultural education; **Primary Target:** all students; **Curricular Aims:** human relations; **Instructional Aims:** multicultural education; **Classroom Environment:** multicultural education; **School Practices:** ESL, culturally diverse faculty, parental involvement in school policy decisions, human relations training for teachers, community involvement in school policy decisions, strong school-community public relations effort, inservice teacher training in multicultural education, Spanish as a second language, student involvement in school policy decisions, interracial student council, human relations training for students, professionally staffed community relations office, professionally staffed human relations team, ethnic studies curriculum; **Groups Studied:** African Americans, Hispanic (Latino/Chicano) Americans, Native Americans; **Element Studied:** literature; **Participating Disciplines:** English, language arts, social studies; **Locally Produced Materials:** yes.

PICKENS COUNTY

Mary Seamon
Director of Curriculum
1348 Griffin Mill Road
Easley, SC 29640
(803) 855-8150 ext. 107

Years In Operation: 2; **Grade Levels:** K-12; **Students Participating:** 1,000; **Community Participation:** community involvement in curriculum planning, use of community resources; **Social Goal:** human relations; **School Goal:** teaching the culturally different; **Primary Target:** all students; **Curricular Aims:** teaching the culturally different; **Instructional Aims:** multicultural/social reconstructionist; **Classroom Environment:** multicultural education; **School Practices:** ESL, remedial classes, culturally diverse faculty, community involvement in school policy decisions, strong school-community public relations effort, student involvement in curriculum planning; **Elements Studied:** art, drama, literature, music.

RICHLAND

Dr. Paul Horne
Social Studies Consultant
Waverley Annex, 1225 Oak Street
Columbia, SC 29204
(803) 733-6176

Years In Operation: 3; **Grade Levels:** K-12; **Students Participating:** 27,000; **Community Participation:** community involvement in curriculum planning, use of community resources, use of human resources in the community, study of the community, interaction with community organizations; **Social Goal:** human relations; **School Goal:** teaching the culturally different; **Primary Target:** all students; **Curricular Aims:** teaching the culturally different; **Instructional Aims:** multicultural education; **Classroom Environment:** multicultural education; **School Practices:** ESL, parental involvement in school policy decisions, human relations training for teachers, community involvement in school policy decisions, strong school-community public relations effort, inservice teacher training in multicultural education, student involvement in school policy decisions, interracial student council, human relations training for students, professionally staffed community relations office.

SOUTH DAKOTA

RAPID CITY
Rosalie A. Bindel, Ph.D.
Instructional Programs
300 Sixth Street
Rapid City, SD 57701
(605) 394-4053

Years In Operation: 22; **Grade Levels:** K-12; **Students Participating:** 1,575; **Community Participation:** community involvement in curriculum planning, use of community resources, use of human resources in the community, interaction with community organizations; **Social Goal:** teaching the culturally different; **School Goal:** human relations; **Primary Target:** minority students; **Curricular Aims:** teaching the culturally different; **Instructional Aims:** multicultural/social reconstructionist; **Classroom Environment:** multicultural/social reconstructionist; **School Practices:** ESL, remedial classes, culturally diverse faculty, parental involvement in school policy decisions, human relations training for teachers, community involvement in school policy decisions, strong school-community public relations effort, Native American language(s); **Group Studied:** Native Americans; **Elements Studied:** art, attitudes, culture and personality, dialect, drama, foods, history, kinship structure, language, literature, music, religion, social customs, values; **Participating Disciplines:** language arts, mathematics, science, social studies.

TENNESSEE

HAMILTON COUNTY
Don Upton
201 Broad Street
Chattanooga, TN 37402
(615) 209-8585

Years In Operation: 12; **Grade Levels:** K-12; **Students Participating:** 212; **Community Participation:** community involvement in curriculum planning, use of human resources in the community, interaction with community organizations; **Social Goal:** multicultural education; **School Goal:** multicultural education; **Primary Target:** all students; **Curricular Aims:** multicultural/social reconstructionist; **Instructional Aims:** multicultural/social reconstructionist; **Classroom Environment:**

multicultural/social reconstructionist; **School Practices:** transitional bilingual education, ESL, remedial classes, culturally diverse staff, human relations training for teachers, community involvement in school policy decisions, inservice teacher training in multicultural education, Spanish as a second language, student involvement in school policy decisions, interracial student council, bilingual curriculum, student human relations council, bicultural curriculum, multilingual curriculum, standard English as a second dialect, Asian language(s), Native American language(s), ethnic studies curriculum; **Groups Studied:** African Americans, Arab Americans, Asian/Pacific Islander Americans, French Americans, German Americans, Greek Americans, Hispanic (Latino/Chicano) Americans, Iranian Americans, Irish Americans, Italian Americans, Native Americans, Portuguese Americans, Scandinavian Americans, Slavic Americans; **Participating Disciplines:** English, foreign languages, health, humanities, physical education, social studies, theater; **Locally Produced Materials:** yes; **Materials Available for Purchase:** yes.

Memphis

Rubbie Patrick-Herring
Bilingual Supervisor
2597 Avery, Room 262
Memphis, TN 38112
(901) 325-5411

Years In Operation: 2; **Grade Levels:** K-12; **Students Participating:** 106,000; **Community Participation:** community involvement in curriculum planning, use of community resources, use of human resources in the community, interaction with community organizations; **Social Goal:** human relations; **School Goal:** human relations; **Primary Target:** all students; **Curricular Aims:** multicultural/social reconstructionist; **Instructional Aims:** multicultural education; **Classroom Environment:** multicultural education; **School Practices:** transitional bilingual education, ESL, remedial classes, parental involvement in school policy decisions, community involvement in school policy decisions, strong school-community public relations effort, inservice teacher training in multicultural education, student involvement in school policy decisions, professionally staffed community relations office; **Locally Produced Materials:** yes.

Shelby County

Dr. Xavier Wynn
Supervisor of Instruction
160 S. Hollywood
Memphis, TN 38115
(901) 325-7900 ext. 623

Years In Operation: 4; **Grade Levels:** K-12; **Students Participating:** 44,000; **Community Participation:** use of community resources, use of human resources in the community, interaction with community organizations; **Social Goal:** multicultural education; **School Goal:** human relations; **Primary Target:** all students; **Curricular**

Aims: human relations; **Instructional Aims:** single-group studies; **Classroom Environment:** multicultural/social reconstructionist; **School Practices:** ESL, culturally diverse staff, human relations training for teachers, community involvement in school policy decisions, strong school-community public relations effort, inservice teacher training in multicultural education, Spanish as a second language, interracial student council, standard English as a second dialect, ethnic studies curriculum; **Group Studied:** African Americans; **Elements Studied:** art, beliefs, culture and personality, foods, history, language, literature, music; **Participating Disciplines:** English, foreign languages, language arts, social studies; **Locally Produced Materials:** yes.

SUMNER COUNTY

Dr. J. Deotha Malone
Supervisor, Secondary Education
225 East Main Street
Gallatin, TN 37066
(615) 451-5227

Years In Operation: 9; **Grade Levels:** K-12; **Students Participating:** 63; **Community Participation:** community involvement in curriculum planning, use of community resources, use of human resources in the community, study of the community, interaction with community organizations; **Social Goal:** teaching the culturally different; **School Goal:** multicultural/social reconstructionist; **Primary Target:** minority students; **Curricular Aims:** teaching the culturally different; **Instructional Aims:** teaching the culturally different; **Classroom Environment:** multicultural/social reconstructionist; **School Practices:** ESL, parental involvement in school policy decisions, human relations training for teachers, strong school-community public relations effort, inservice teacher training in multicultural education, interracial student council, human relations training for students, bilingual curriculum, student human relations council, multilingual curriculum, standard English as a second dialect, ethnic studies curriculum; **Groups Studied:** African Americans, Asian/Pacific Islander Americans, German Americans, Native Americans; **Elements Studied:** art, attitudes, beliefs, culture and personality, dialect, drama, foods, kinship structure, language, literature, music, religion, social customs, social organization, social structure, values; **Participating Disciplines:** art, English, foreign languages, health, home economics, language arts, mathematics, music, physical education, reading, social studies, theater.

WILSON COUNTY
Felicia Duncan
Elementary Supervisor of Instruction
501 B Park Avenue
Lebanon, TN 37087
(615) 443-8719

Years In Operation: 5; **Grade Levels:** K-12; **Students Participating:** 35,000; **Community Participation:** community involvement in curriculum planning, use of community resources, use of human resources in the community, a community based instructional program, study of the community, interaction with community organizations; **Social Goal:** human relations; **School Goal:** human relations; **Primary Target:** all students; **Curricular Aims:** multicultural education; **Instructional Aims:** multicultural/social reconstructionist; **Classroom Environment:** human relations, single-group studies; **School Practices:** transitional bilingual education, ESL, remedial classes, culturally diverse faculty, parental involvement in school policy decisions, culturally diverse staff, human relations training for teachers, community involvement in school policy decisions, strong school-community public relations effort, inservice teacher training in multicultural education, student involvement in curriculum planning, Spanish as a second language, student involvement in school policy decisions, interracial student council, human relations training for students, professionally staffed community relations office, bilingual curriculum, professionally staffed human relations team, student human relations council, bicultural curriculum, multilingual curriculum, standard English as a second dialect, Asian language(s), Native American language(s), ethnic studies curriculum; **Groups Studied:** African Americans, Arab Americans, Asian/Pacific Islander Americans, Hispanic (Latino/Chicano) Americans, Native Americans; **Elements Studied:** art, beliefs, body language, culture and personality, drama, foods, history, kinship structure, language, literature, material culture, music, religion, social customs, social organization, social structure, values; **Participating Disciplines:** art, English, foreign languages, humanities, language arts, music, reading, social studies; **Locally Produced Materials:** yes.

TEXAS

ALIEF
Greg Byers/Judy Wallis
Social Studies Coordinators
P.O. Box 68
Alief, TX 77411
(713) 498-8110

Years In Operation: 7; **Grade Levels:** K-12; **Students Participating:** 35,000; **Community Participation:** community involvement in curriculum planning, use of community resources, use of human resources in the community, a community based instructional program, study of the community, interaction with community organiza-

tions; **Social Goal:** human relations; **School Goal:** multicultural education; **Primary Target:** all students; **Curricular Aims:** multicultural education; **Instructional Aims:** multicultural/social reconstructionist; **Classroom Environment:** single-group studies; **School Practices:** transitional bilingual education, ESL, remedial classes, culturally diverse faculty, parental involvement in school policy decisions, culturally diverse staff, human relations training for teachers, community involvement in school policy decisions, strong school-community public relations effort, inservice teacher training in multicultural education, student involvement in curricular planning, Spanish as a second language, student involvement in school policy decisions, interracial student council, human relations training for students, professionally staffed community relations office, bilingual curriculum, professionally staffed human relations team, student human relations council, bicultural curriculum, multilingual curriculum, standard English as a second dialect, ethnic studies curriculum; **Groups Studied:** African Americans, Arab Americans, Asian/Pacific Islander Americans, Hispanic (Latino/Chicano) Americans, Native Americans; **Elements Studied:** art, beliefs, body language, culture and personality, drama, foods, history, kinship structure, language, literature, material culture, music, religion, social customs, social organization, social structure, values; **Participating Disciplines:** art, English, foreign languages, humanities, language arts, music, reading, social studies; **Locally Produced Materials:** yes.

ARLINGTON
Vanyelle Williams
1203 West Pioneer Parkway
Arlington, TX 76013
(817) 460-4611

Years In Operation: 12; **Grade Levels:** K-12; **Students Participating:** 50,150; **Community Participation:** community involvement in curriculum planning, use of community resources, use of human resources in the community, interaction with community organizations; **Social Goal:** human relations; **School Goal:** human relations; **Primary Target:** all students; **Curricular Aims:** human relations; **Instructional Aims:** multicultural education; **Classroom Environment:** multicultural education; **School Practices:** transitional bilingual education, ESL, remedial classes, culturally diverse faculty, parental involvement in school policy decisions, culturally diverse staff, human relations training for teachers, community involvement in school policy decisions, strong school-community public relations effort, inservice teacher training in multicultural education, student involvement in curriculum planning, Spanish as a second language, student involvement in school policy decisions, interracial student council, professionally staffed community relations office, bilingual curriculum, professionally staffed human relations team, multilingual curriculum, standard English as a second dialect; **Elements Studied:** art, beliefs, culture and personality, drama, foods, history, language, literature, music, religion, social customs, social organization; **Participating Disciplines:** art, English, foreign languages, humanities, language arts, social studies; **Locally Produced Materials:** yes.

Carrollton-Farmers Branch
Dr. Barbara Caffee
Instructional Coordinator
P.O. Box 115186
Carrollton, TX 75011
(214) 323-5744

Conroe
James E. Ferguson
Director of Curriculum & Instructional Services
702 North Thompson Street
Conroe, TX 77301
(409) 760-7785

Grade Levels: K-12; **Students Participating:** 28,000; **Social Goal:** single-group studies; **Primary Target:** all students; **Curricular Aims:** multicultural/social reconstructionist; **Classroom Environment:** multicultural/social reconstructionist; **School Practices:** transitional bilingual education, ESL, culturally diverse faculty, parental involvement in school policy decisions, culturally diverse staff, human relations training for teachers, community involvement in school policy decisions, strong school-community public relations effort, inservice teacher training in multicultural education, Spanish as a second language, human relations training for students, professionally staffed community relations office, bilingual curriculum, student human relations council, multilingual curriculum, Asian language(s); **Elements Studied:** art, attitudes, culture and personality, foods, history, language, literature, music, social customs, social organization, social structure.

Cypress-Fairbanks
Pam Wells
Director of Instruction
22602 Hempstead Highway
Cypress, TX 77429
(713) 897-4643

Dallas
Dr. Doris Freeling
Director, Social Studies Education
3700 Ross Avenue, Box 103
Dallas, TX 75204
(214) 989-8358

DEER PARK
Bobby Grisham
Coordinator, Multicultural Programs & Assistant Superintendent
210 Ivy Avenue
Deer Park, TX 77536
(713) 930-4606

Years In Operation: 2; **Grade Levels:** K-12; **Students Participating:** 1,000; **Community Participation:** community involvement in curriculum planning, use of community resources, use of human resources in the community, interaction with community organizations; **Social Goal:** human relations; **School Goal:** human relations; **Primary Target:** all students; **Curricular Aims:** human relations; **Instructional Aims:** teaching the culturally different; **Classroom Environment:** multicultural/social reconstructionist; **School Practices:** transitional bilingual education, ESL, remedial classes, culturally diverse faculty, parental involvement in school policy decisions, culturally diverse staff, human relations training for teachers, community involvement in school policy decisions, strong school-community public relations effort, inservice teacher training in multicultural education, Spanish as a second language, student involvement in school policy decisions, interracial student council, human relations training for students, professionally staffed community relations office, bilingual curriculum, professionally staffed human relations team, bicultural curriculum, Asian language(s), Native American language(s), ethnic studies curriculum; **Groups Studied:** African Americans, Asian/Pacific Islander Americans, Hispanic (Latino/Chicano) Americans, Native Americans; **Elements Studied:** art, attitudes, beliefs, body language, culture and personality, dialect, drama, foods, history, kinship structure, language, literature, material culture, music, physical characteristics, religion, social customs, social organization, social structure, values; **Participating Disciplines:** art, business, English, foreign languages, health, home economics, humanities, industrial arts, language arts, mathematics, music, physical education, reading, science, social studies, theater; **Locally Produced Materials:** yes.

DUNCANVILLE
Dr. Cathy Bryce
Assistant Superintendent for Curriculum & Instruction
502 East Freeman
Duncanville, TX 75116
(214) 709-2961

Years In Operation: 1; **Grade Levels:** K-12; **Students Participating:** 10,000; **Community Participation:** community involvement in curriculum planning, use of community resources, use of human resources in the community, a community based instructional program, study of the community, interaction with community organizations; **Social Goal:** human relations; **School Goal:** human relations; **Primary Target:** all students; **Curricular Aims:** multicultural education; **Instructional Aims:** multicultural/social reconstructionist; **Classroom Environment:** multicultural/social reconstructionist; **School Practices:** ESL, remedial classes, culturally diverse faculty, parental involvement in school policy decisions, culturally diverse staff, human relations training for teachers, community involvement in school policy decisions, strong school-community public relations effort, inservice teacher training in multicultural education, student involvement in school policy decisions, interracial student council, human relations training for students, professionally staffed community relations office, ethnic studies curriculum; **Groups Studied:** African Americans, Hispanic (Latino/Chicano) Americans; **Elements Studied:** art, attitudes, beliefs, body language, culture and personality, dialect, drama, foods, history, kinship structure, language, literature, religion, social customs, social organization, social structure, values; **Participating Disciplines:** art, English, foreign languages, language arts, music, reading, science, social studies, theater.

EL PASO

Argelia Carreon
Director, Accelerated Bilingual Education Program
6531 Boeing Drive
El Paso, TX 79925
(915) 779-4139

Years In Operation: 3; **Grade Levels:** K-5; **Students Participating:** 360; **Community Participation:** a community based instructional program, study of the community, interaction with community organizations, Parents As Partners in Education; **Social Goal:** multicultural education; **School Goal:** multicultural education; **Primary Target:** all students; **Curricular Aims:** multicultural education; **Instructional Aims:** multicultural education; **Classroom Environment:** single-group studies; **School Practices:** transitional bilingual education, parental involvement in school policy decisions, inservice teacher training in multicultural education, Spanish as a second language, bilingual curriculum, bicultural curriculum, multilingual curriculum; **Locally Produced Materials:** yes.

FORT BEND

Dr. Holly Dale
Associate Superintendent
P.O. Box 1004
Sugarland, TX 77478
(713) 980-1300

Grade Levels: K-12; **Students Participating:** 40,614; **Community Participation:** use of community resources, a community based instructional program, study of the community, interaction with community organizations; **Social Goal:** single-group studies; **School Goal:** multicultural education; **Primary Target:** all students; **Curricular Aims:** multicultural/social reconstructionist; **Instructional Aims:** multicultural/social reconstructionist; **Classroom Environment:** multicultural/social reconstructionist; **School Practices:** transitional bilingual education, ESL, remedial classes, culturally diverse faculty, parental involvement in school policy decisions, culturally diverse staff, human relations training for teachers, community involvement in school policy decisions, strong school-community public relations effort, inservice teacher training in multicultural education, Spanish as a second language, interracial student council, human relations training for students, professionally staffed community relations office, bilingual curriculum, professionally staffed human relations team, bicultural curriculum, ethnic studies curriculum; **Groups Studied:** African Americans, Asian/Pacific Islander Americans, Hispanic (Latino/Chicano) Americans; **Elements Studied:** attitudes, beliefs, culture and personality, foods, history, language, literature, music, religion, social customs; **Participating Disciplines:** art, English, foreign languages, language arts, reading.

FORT WORTH

Joyce Howard Johnson
Program Director, Social Studies
100 North University, SW 210
Fort Worth, TX 76107
(817) 871-2513

GALENA PARK

Vernon Cannamore
Social Studies Coordinator
P.O. Box 565
Galena Park, TX 77547
(713) 672-7491 ext. 257

Years In Operation: 3; **Grade Levels:** 1-12; **Students Participating:** 15,000; **Community Participation:** use of community resources, use of human resources in the community, a community based instructional program, study of the community; **Social Goal:** human relations; **School Goal:** human relations; **Primary Target:** all students; **Curricular Aims:** multicultural/social reconstructionist; **Instructional Aims:** multicultural/social reconstructionist; **Classroom Environment:** human relations, single-group studies; **School Practices:** ESL, remedial classes, culturally diverse faculty, parental involvement in school policy decisions, community involvement in school policy decisions, inservice teacher training in multicultural education, Spanish as a second language, student involvement in school policy decisions, interracial student council, bilingual curriculum, bicultural curriculum, standard English as a second dialect, ethnic studies curriculum; **Groups Studied:** African Americans, Hispanic (Latino/ Chicano) Americans; **Elements Studied:** culture and personality, history, language, music, physical characteristics, religion, social customs, values; **Participating Disciplines:** language arts, social studies.

GRAND PRAIRIE
Rudy Lopez
Director of Multicultural Education/Secondary ESL
202 College Street
Grand Prairie, TX 75050
(214) 264-6141 ext. 301

Years In Operation: 1; **Grade Levels:** K-12; **Students Participating:** 17,500; **Community Participation:** use of human resources in the community, a community based instructional program; **Social Goal:** multicultural education; **School Goal:** multicultural education; **Primary Target:** all students; **Curricular Aims:** multicultural/social reconstructionist; **Instructional Aims:** multicultural/social reconstructionist; **Classroom Environment:** multicultural/social reconstructionist; **School Practices:** transitional bilingual education, ESL, culturally diverse faculty, culturally diverse staff, human relations training for teachers, strong school-community public relations effort, inservice teacher training in multicultural education, human relations training for students, bilingual curriculum, bicultural curriculum, standard English as a second dialect; **Elements Studied:** beliefs, foods, history, music, social customs, social structure, values.

GRAPEVINE-COLLEYVILLE
Suzy Hagar
Instructional Coordinator
3051 Ira East Woods Avenue
Grapevine, TX 76051
(817) 481-5575 ext. 473

HOUSTON
Marthea Raney
Principal, Turner Elementary School
3200 Rosedale
Houston, TX 77004
(713) 942-1490

Years In Operation: 22; **Grade Levels:** K-6,9; **Students Participating:** 13,000; **Community Participation:** use of community resources, use of human resources in the community, interaction with community organizations; **Social Goal:** human relations; **School Goal:** human relations; **Primary Target:** all students; **Curricular Aims:** human relations; **Instructional Aims:** human relations; **Classroom Environment:** single-group studies; **School Practices:** culturally diverse faculty, human relations training for teachers, strong school-community public relations effort, inservice teacher training in multicultural education; **Elements Studied:** art, beliefs, culture and personality, foods, history, language, literature, music, physical characteristics, social customs, values.

HUMBLE

Elizabeth Pearson Walker
Coordinator of Special Programs
P.O. Box 2000
Humble, TX 77347
(713) 540-5934

Years In Operation: 8; **Grade Levels:** K-12; **Students Participating:** 7,000; **Community Participation:** use of community resources, use of human resources in the community, study of the community; **Social Goal:** multicultural education; **School Goal:** multicultural /social reconstructionist; **Primary Target:** all students; **Curricular Aims:** multicultural education; **Instructional Aims:** multicultural/social reconstructionist; **Classroom Environment:** multicultural/social reconstructionist; **School Practices:** transitional bilingual education, ESL, remedial classes, parental involvement in school policy decisions, culturally diverse staff, human relations training for teachers, community involvement in school policy decisions, strong school-community public relations effort, inservice teacher training in multicultural education, student involvement in curriculum planning, Spanish as a second language, student involvement in school policy decisions, interracial student council, human relations training for students, professionally staffed community relations office, bilingual curriculum, multilingual curriculum, ethnic studies curriculum; **Groups Studied:** African Americans, Asian/Pacific Islander Americans, Hispanic (Latino/Chicano) Americans, Irish Americans, Italian Americans; **Elements Studied:** art, attitudes, beliefs, culture and personality, drama, foods, history, kinship structure, language, literature, material culture, music, physical characteristics, religion, social customs, social organization, social structure, values; **Participating Disciplines:** art, English, health, language arts, mathematics, music, physical education, reading, science, social studies.

KATY

Maydel Jenks
Instructional Officer
6301 South Stadium Lane
Katy, TX 77494
(713) 391-2184 ext. 377

Years In Operation: 4; **Grade Levels:** K-12; **Students Participating:** 1,000; **Community Participation:** community involvement in curriculum planning, use of community resources; **Social Goal:** human relations; **School Goal:** human relations; **Primary Target:** all students; **Curricular Aims:** multicultural education; **Instructional Aims:** multicultural/social reconstructionist; **Classroom Environment:** multicultural/social reconstructionist; **School Practices:** transitional bilingual education, ESL, parental involvement in school policy decisions, community involvement in school policy decisions, inservice teacher training in multicultural education, Spanish as a second language, student involvement in school policy decisions, interracial student council, bilingual curriculum, standard English as a second dialect, Asian language(s); **Elements Studied:** art, beliefs, foods, history, kinship structure, language, music, social customs.

KILLEEN
Dr. Mary Keller
Assistant Superintendent for Education Services
200 North W.S. Young, P.O. Box 967
Killeen, TX 76540-0967
(817) 520-1358

KLEIN
Dr. Nancy Radcliffe
Director of Instruction
7200 Spring Cypress Road
Klein, TX 77379-3299
(713) 376-4180 ext. 235

MESQUITE
Glenda Heil
Administrative Curriculum Officer
405 East Davis
Mesquite, TX 75145
(214) 882-7441

MIDLAND
Patty Smith
Coordinator of Social Studies
615 West Missouri Avenue, Suite 520
Midland, TX 79701
(915) 689-1017

Years In Operation: 4; **Grade Levels:** K-12; **Community Participation:** use of human resources in the community; **Social Goal:** human relations; **School Goal:** teaching the culturally different; **Primary Target:** all students; **Curricular Aims:** human relations; **Instructional Aims:** human relations; **Classroom Environment:** teaching the culturally different, single-group studies; **School Practices:** culturally diverse faculty, human relations training for teachers, community involvement in school policy decisions, strong school-community public relations effort, inservice teacher training in multicultural education, ethnic studies curriculum; **Groups Studied:** African Americans, Arab Americans, Asian/Pacific Islander Americans, German Americans, Hispanic (Latino/Chicano) Americans, Irish Americans, Italian Americans, Native Americans; **Elements Studied:** attitudes, beliefs, culture and personality, drama, history, literature, physical characteristics, religion, social customs, values; **Participating Disciplines:** English, social studies; **Locally Produced Materials:** yes; **Materials Available for Purchase:** seven secondary social studies courses ($250 per course).

NORTH EAST
Chula Boyle
Principal
1400 Jackson Keller
San Antonio, TX 78213
(210) 442-0404

NORTHSIDE
Mike Watts
590 Evers Road
San Antonio, TX 78238
(512) 647-2288

Years In Operation: 2; **Grade Levels:** 11-12; **Students Participating:** 60; **Community Participation:** use of human resources in the community, interaction with community organizations; **Social Goal:** single-group studies; **School Goal:** teaching the culturally different; **Primary Target:** all students; **Curricular Aims:** single-group studies; **Instructional Aims:** single-group studies; **School Practices:** ESL, community involvement in school policy decisions, strong school-community public relations effort, interracial student council, professionally staffed community relations office, bilingual curriculum, ethnic studies curriculum; **Groups Studied:** African Americans, Hispanic (Latino/Chicano) Americans, Native Americans; **Elements Studied:** art, attitudes, beliefs, body language, culture and personality, dialect, drama, foods, history, kinship structure, language, literature, material culture, music, physical characteristics, religion, social customs, social organization, social structure, values; **Participating Discipline:** social studies.

PASADENA
Gloria Gallegos
Director of Special Programs
1515 Cherrybrook
Pasadena, TX 77502
(713) 920-6923

PORT ARTHUR
Charlie Vanatta
Assistant Superintendent
P.O. Box 1388
Port Arthur, TX 77641-1388
(409) 989-6257

SPRING

Mary Lynn Johnson
Program Director for Social Studies
18717 Ella Boulevard
Houston, TX 77090
(713) 586-1113

Years In Operation: 2; **Grade Levels:** K-12; **Students Participating:** 2,000; **Community Participation:** use of community resources, use of human resources in the community, interaction with community organizations; **Social Goal:** human relations; **School Goal:** multicultural/social reconstructionist; **Primary Target:** all students; **Curricular Aims:** multicultural education; **Instructional Aims:** multicultural/social reconstructionist; **Classroom Environment:** multicultural/social reconstructionist; **School Practices:** ESL, culturally diverse faculty, parental involvement in school policy decisions, culturally diverse staff, human relations training for teachers, community involvement in school policy decisions, strong school-community public relations effort, inservice teacher training in multicultural education, student involvement in curriculum planning, Spanish as a second language, student involvement in school policy decisions, interracial student council, human relations training for students, professionally staffed community relations office, bilingual curriculum.

UTAH

ALPINE

Dr. Victoria Anderson
Director, Pupil Services
575 North 100 East
American Fork, UT 84003
(801) 756-8400

Grade Levels: K-12; **Community Participation:** community involvement in curriculum planning, use of human resources in the community, interaction with community organizations; **Social Goal:** multicultural education; **School Goal:** multicultural education; **Primary Target:** minority students; **Curricular Aims:** teaching the culturally different; **Instructional Aims:** multicultural/social reconstructionist; **Classroom Environment:** single-group studies; **School Practices:** transitional bilingual education, ESL, human relations training for teachers, community involvement in school policy decisions, strong school-community public relations effort, inservice teacher training in multicultural education, Spanish as a second language, student involvement in school policy decisions, human relations training for students, bicultural curriculum, standard English as a second dialect.

GRANITE

Ike Spencer
Associate Director, Multicultural Education
340 East 3545 South
Salt Lake, UT 84115
(801) 268-8582

Years In Operation: 23; **Grade Levels:** K-12; **Students Participating:** 80,102; **Community Participation:** use of community resources, use of human resources in the community, interaction with community organizations, parenting group; **Social Goal:** human relations; **School Goal:** multicultural education; **Primary Target:** all students; **Curricular Aims:** multicultural education; **Instructional Aims:** multicultural education; **Classroom Environment:** multicultural/social reconstructionist; **School Practices:** ESL, remedial classes, inservice teacher training in multicultural education, ethnic studies curriculum; **Groups Studied:** African Americans, Asian/Pacific Islander Americans, German Americans, Greek Americans, Hispanic (Latino/Chicano) Americans, Irish Americans, Native Americans; **Elements Studied:** art, beliefs, culture and personality, history, language, literature, music; **Participating Disciplines:** art, English, language arts, music, social studies; **Locally Produced Materials:** yes.

JORDAN

Dr. Ilona Pierce
Director of Instructional Support Services
9361 South 300 East
Sandy, UT 84070
(801) 567-8296

Years In Operation: 16; **Grade Levels:** K-12; **Students Participating:** 1,159; **Community Participation:** community involvement in curriculum planning, interaction with community organizations, parent committee; **Social Goal:** single-group studies; **School Goal:** multicultural education; **Primary Target:** minority students; **Curricular Aims:** teaching the culturally different; **Instructional Aims:** teaching the culturally different; **School Practices:** ESL, inservice teacher training in multicultural education, multilingual curriculum.

NEBO

Nedra Call
International Education
350 South Main
Spanish Fork, UT 84660
(801) 798-4021

Years In Operation: 6; **Grade Levels:** K-12; **Students Participating:** 600; **Social Goal:** teaching the culturally different; **School Goal:** human relations; **Primary Target:** all students; **Curricular Aims:** multicultural education; **Instructional Aims:**

multicultural education; **Classroom Environment:** human relations; **School Practices:** transitional bilingual education, ESL, remedial classes, parental involvement in school policy decisions, human relations training for teachers, community involvement in school policy decisions, strong school-community public relations effort, inservice teacher training in multicultural education, Spanish as a second language, human relations training for students, Asian language(s); **Elements Studied:** art, attitudes, beliefs, culture and personality, foods, history, kinship structure, language, literature, music, physical characteristics, religion, social customs, social organization, social structure; **Locally Produced Materials:** yes.

Ogden

Santiago Sandoval
Director of Cultural Diversity
1950 Monroe
Ogden, UT 84401
(801) 625-1153

Weber

Lynne Greenwood
Multicultural Education
5320 South Adams Avenue
Ogden, UT 84405
(801) 476-7875

Grade Levels: K-12; **Students Participating:** 28,000; **Community Participation:** community involvement in curriculum planning, use of community resources, use of human resources in the community, a community based instructional program, interaction with community organizations; **Social Goal:** multicultural education; **School Goal:** multicultural/social reconstructionist; **Primary Target:** all students; **Curricular Aims:** multicultural/social reconstructionist; **Instructional Aims:** multicultural/ social reconstructionist; **Classroom Environment:** multicultural/social reconstructionist; **School Practices:** transitional bilingual education, ESL, remedial classes, culturally diverse faculty, parental involvement in school policy decisions, culturally diverse staff, human relations training for teachers, community involvement in school policy decisions, strong school-community public relations effort, inservice teacher training in multicultural education, student involvement in curriculum planning, Spanish as a second language, student involvement in school policy decisions, interracial student council, human relations training for students, student human relations council, bicultural curriculum, multilingual curriculum, standard English as a second dialect, ethnic studies curriculum; **Groups Studied:** African Americans, Arab Americans, Asian/Pacific Islander Americans, French Americans, German Americans, Greek Americans, Hispanic (Latino/Chicano) Americans, Iranian Americans, Irish Americans, Italian Americans, Native Americans, Portuguese Americans, Scandinavian Americans, Slavic Americans; **Elements Studied:** art, attitudes, beliefs, drama, foods, history, kinship structure, language, literature, material culture, music, religion, social customs, social structure, values; **Participating Disciplines:** art, English, foreign languages, humanities, language arts, music, reading, science, social studies, theater.

VIRGINIA

CHESAPEAKE
G. Charlene Chappell
Supervisor of Social Studies/Humanities
300 Cedar Road
Chesapeake, VA 23320
(804) 547-0153 ext. 186

HENRICO COUNTY
Thomas Bailey
P.O. Box 23120
Richmond, VA 23223
(804) 226-3717

Grade Levels: K-12; **Community Participation:** use of community resources, use of human resources in the community, study of the community, interaction with community organizations; **Social Goal:** multicultural education; **School Goal:** multicultural education; **Primary Target:** all students; **Curricular Aims:** multicultural/social reconstructionist; **Instructional Aims:** multicultural/social reconstructionist; **Classroom Environment:** single-group studies; **School Practices:** transitional bilingual education, ESL, remedial classes, culturally diverse faculty, parental involvement in school policy decisions, culturally diverse staff, human relations training for teachers, community involvement in school policy decisions, strong school-community public relations effort, inservice teacher training in multicultural education, student involvement in curriculum planning, Spanish as a second language, student involvement in school policy decisions, interracial student council, human relations training for students, professionally staffed community relations office, Asian language(s).

LOUDOUN COUNTY
Dr. Thomas Woodall
Instructional Supervisor, Social Studies & Gifted Education
102 North Street NW
Leesburg, VA 22075
(703) 771-6435

Years In Operation: 6; **Grade Levels:** K-12; **Students Participating:** 16,000; **Community Participation:** community involvement in curriculum planning, use of community resources, use of human resources in the community, study of the community, interaction with community organizations; **Social Goal:** human relations; **School Goal:** human relations; **Primary Target:** all students; **Curricular Aims:** multicultural education; **Instructional Aims:** multicultural education; **Classroom Environment:** multicultural/social reconstructionist; **School Practices:** ESL, culturally diverse faculty, parental involvement in school policy decisions, culturally diverse staff, human relations training for teachers, community involvement in school policy decisions, strong school-community public relations effort, inservice teacher training in multicultural education, student involvement in curriculum planning, student involvement in school policy decisions, human relations training for students, professionally staffed community relations office, standard English as a second dialect, ethnic studies curriculum; **Groups Studied:** African Americans, Arab Americans, Asian/Pacific Islander Americans, French Americans, German Americans, Greek Americans, Hispanic (Latino/Chicano) Americans, Irish Americans, Italian Americans, Native Americans; **Elements Studied:** art, beliefs, culture and personality, foods, history, language, literature, material culture, music, religion, social customs, social structure; **Participating Disciplines:** art, English, foreign languages, language arts, music, physical education, reading, science, social studies; **Locally Produced Materials:** yes.

NORFOLK

Brenda P. Shepherd
Multicultural Specialist
800 East City Hall Avenue
Norfolk, VA 23501
(804) 441-2859

PORTSMOUTH CITY

Claude C. Parent
Director of Instruction
3651 Hartford Street
Portsmouth, VA 23707
(804) 393-8555

Years In Operation: 1; **Grade Levels:** K-12; **Students Participating:** 500; **Community Participation:** study of the community, interaction with community organizations; **Social Goal:** multicultural education; **School Goal:** multicultural/social reconstructionist; **Primary Target:** minority students; **Curricular Aims:** teaching the culturally different; **Instructional Aims:** multicultural/social reconstructionist; **Classroom Environment:** multicultural/social reconstructionist; **School Practices:** transitional bilingual education, ESL, remedial classes, parental involvement in school policy decisions, culturally diverse staff, human relations training for teachers, community involvement in school policy decisions, strong school-community public relations effort, inservice teacher training in multicultural education, human relations training for students, professionally staffed human relations team, Asian language(s), ethnic studies curriculum; **Groups Studied:** African Americans, Asian/Pacific Islander Americans, French Americans, German Americans, Greek Americans, Hispanic

(Latino/Chicano) Americans, Irish Americans, Italian Americans, Native Americans, Portuguese Americans, Scandinavian Americans; **Elements Studied:** art, attitudes, beliefs, culture and personality, dialect, drama, foods, history, kinship structure, language, literature, material culture, music, physical characteristics, social customs, social organization, social structure, values; **Participating Disciplines:** art, business, English, foreign languages, health, home economics, humanities, industrial arts, language arts, mathematics, music, physical education, reading, science, social studies, theater.

PRINCE WILLIAM COUNTY
Larry Bell
Supervisor, Multicultural Education
14800 Joplin Road
Manassas, VA 22110
(703) 791-7270

Years In Operation: 3; **Grade Levels:** K-12; **Students Participating:** 46,000; **Community Participation:** use of community resources, use of human resources in the community, interaction with community organizations, multicultural advisory committee; **Social Goal:** teaching the culturally different; **School Goal:** teaching the culturally different; **Primary Target:** all students; **Curricular Aims:** teaching the culturally different; **Instructional Aims:** teaching the culturally different; **Classroom Environment:** multicultural education; **School Practices:** transitional bilingual education, ESL, culturally diverse staff, human relations training for teachers, community involvement in school policy decisions, strong school-community public relations effort, inservice teacher training in multicultural education, Spanish as a second language, professionally staffed community relations office, ethnic studies curriculum; **Groups Studied:** African Americans, Arab Americans, Asian/Pacific Islander Americans, Hispanic (Latino/Chicano) Americans, Native Americans; **Elements Studied:** art, attitudes, beliefs, body language, culture and personality, dialect, drama, foods, history, kinship structure, language, literature, material culture, music, physical characteristics, religion, social customs, social organization, social structure, values; **Participating Disciplines:** art, social studies; **Locally Produced Materials:** yes.

RICHMOND CITY
Oneida Pozier
Social Studies Specialist
301 North 9th Street
Richmond, VA 23219
(804) 780-7765

Years In Operation: 5; **Grade Levels:** K-12; **Students Participating:** 24,000; **Community Participation:** use of community resources, use of human resources in the community, interaction with community organizations; **Social Goal:** teaching the culturally different; **School Goal:** teaching the culturally different; **Primary Target:** all students; **Curricular Aims:** multicultural education; **Instructional Aims:** multicultural education; **Classroom Environment:** single-group studies; **School Practices:** ESL, remedial classes, culturally diverse faculty, parental involvement in school policy decisions, culturally diverse staff, community involvement in school policy decisions, strong school-community public relations effort, inservice teacher training in multicultural education, Spanish as a second language, professionally staffed community relations office, bicultural curriculum, ethnic studies curriculum; **Group Studied:** African Americans; **Elements Studied:** art, beliefs, body language, culture and personality, foods, history, language, literature, material culture, music, religion, social customs, social organization, social structure; **Participating Disciplines:** art, English, foreign languages, language arts, mathematics, music, science, social studies; **Locally Produced Materials:** yes.

ROANOKE COUNTY
David Wymer
Supervisor of Social Studies
5937 Cove Road NW
Roanoke, VA 24019
(540) 562-3725

Years In Operation: 6; **Grade Levels:** K-12; **Students Participating:** 13,000; **Community Participation:** community involvement in curriculum planning, use of community resources, use of human resources in the community, study of the community, interaction with community organizations; **Social Goal:** human relations; **School Goal:** human relations; **Primary Target:** all students; **Curricular Aims:** multicultural/social reconstructionist; **Instructional Aims:** human relations; **Classroom Environment:** multicultural/social reconstructionist; **School Practices:** ESL, remedial classes, parental involvement in school policy decisions, human relations training for teachers, community involvement in school policy decisions, strong school-community public relations effort, inservice teacher training in multicultural education, student involvement in school policy decisions, human relations training for students, ethnic studies curriculum; **Groups Studied:** African Americans, Arab Americans, Asian/Pacific Islander Americans, Hispanic (Latino/Chicano) Americans, Iranian Americans, Native Americans; **Elements Studied:** art, beliefs, culture and personality, history, literature, physical characteristics, religion, social customs, social organization; **Participating Disciplines:** art, English, foreign languages, language arts, social studies; **Locally Produced Materials:** yes.

WASHINGTON

AUBURN
Tim Cummings
Director of Curriculum
915 Fourth Street NE
Auburn, WA 98002
(206) 931-4923

Years In Operation: 11; **Grade Levels:** K-12; **Students Participating:** 12,000; **Community Participation:** community involvement in curriculum planning, use of community resources, use of human resources in the community, interaction with community organizations, cultural diversity committee; **Social Goal:** human relations; **School Goal:** human relations; **Primary Target:** all students; **Curricular Aims:** multicultural education; **Instructional Aims:** multicultural education; **Classroom Environment:** multicultural/social reconstructionist; **School Practices:** transitional bilingual education, ESL, remedial classes, culturally diverse faculty, parental involvement in school policy decisions, community involvement in school policy decisions, strong school-community public relations effort, inservice teacher training in multicultural education, interracial student council, bilingual curriculum, standard English as a second dialect.

BETHEL
Mary Jo Riese
Teacher of Cultural Diversity
Bethel High School
East 38th Ave.
Spanaway, WA 98387
(206) 846-9710
Tim Sullivan
Facilitator
Spanaway Lake High School
Spanaway, WA 98387
(206) 535-2972

Years In Operation: 8; **Grade Levels:** 6, 9-12; **Students Participating:** 175; **Community Participation:** use of community resources, use of human resources in the community, interaction with community organizations; **Social Goal:** human relations; **School Goal:** human relations; **Primary Target:** all students; **Curricular Aims:** teaching the culturally different; **Instructional Aims:** multicultural/social reconstructionist; **Classroom Environment:** multicultural/social reconstructionist; **School Practices:** culturally diverse faculty, community involvement in school policy decisions, student involvement in school policy decisions, human relations training for students, professionally staffed community relations office, ethnic studies curriculum; **Groups Stud-**

ied: African Americans, Asian/Pacific Islander Americans, German Americans, Hispanic (Latino/Chicano) Americans, Irish Americans, Italian Americans, Native Americans, Scandinavian Americans, Slavic Americans; **Elements Studied:** art, attitudes, beliefs, body language, culture and personality, drama, foods, history, literature, music, physical characteristics, religion, social customs, social structure, values; **Participating Disciplines:** art, English, health, humanities, language arts, reading, science, social studies.

CLOVER PARK
Kathy Lemmer
Director of Curriculum
10903 Gravelly Lake Drive SW
Tacoma, WA 98499
(206) 589-7411

Years In Operation: 10; **Grade Levels:** K-12; **Students Participating:** 13,000; **Community Participation:** use of community resources, use of human resources in the community, interaction with community organizations; **Social Goal:** multicultural education; **School Goal:** human relations; **Primary Target:** all students; **Curricular Aims:** teaching the culturally different; **Instructional Aims:** multicultural education; **Classroom Environment:** human relations, single-group studies; **School Practices:** ESL, remedial classes, culturally diverse faculty, parental involvement in school policy decisions, culturally diverse staff, community involvement in school policy decisions, strong school-community public relations effort, inservice teacher training in multicultural education, Spanish as a second language, student involvement in school policy decisions, interracial student council, human relations training for students, professionally staffed community relations office, student human relations council, standard English as a second dialect, Asian language(s); **Locally Produced Materials:** yes.

EDMONDS
Marcia Migdal
Coordinator of Multicultural Education
20420 68th Avenue West
Lynnwood, WA 98036
(206) 670-7128

EVERGREEN
Evie Grendahl
Director of Curriculum
13501 NE 28th Street
Vancouver, WA 98682
(206) 256-6000

Community Participation: community involvement in curriculum planning, use of community resources, use of human resources in the community, interaction with community organizations; **Social Goal:** multicultural education; **School Goal:** multicultural education; **Primary Target:** all students; **Curricular Aims:** multicultural education; **Instructional Aims:** multicultural education; **Classroom Environment:** multicultural education; **School Practices:** transitional bilingual education, ESL, remedial classes, culturally diverse faculty, parental involvement in school policy decisions, culturally diverse staff, human relations training for teachers, community involvement in school policy decisions, strong school-community public relations effort, inservice teacher training in multicultural education, Spanish as a second language, student involvement in school policy decisions, professionally staffed community relations office, standard English as a second dialect; **Locally Produced Materials:** yes.

KENNEWICK
Vicki Rynd
Federal Projects Coordinator
200 South Dayton
Kennewick, WA 99336
(509) 736-2667

Years In Operation: 8; **Grade Levels:** K-12; **Students Participating:** 12,399; **Community Participation:** community involvement in curriculum planning, use of community resources, use of human resources in the community, interaction with community organizations; **Social Goal:** multicultural education; **School Goal:** multicultural education; **Primary Target:** all students; **Curricular Aims:** multicultural education; **Instructional Aims:** multicultural education; **Classroom Environment:** multicultural education; **School Practices:** transitional bilingual education, ESL, remedial classes, culturally diverse faculty, parental involvement in school policy decisions, human relations training for teachers, community involvement in school policy decisions, strong school-community public relations effort, inservice teacher training in multicultural education, Spanish as a second language, interracial student council, professionally staffed community relations office, bilingual curriculum, professionally staffed human relations team, bicultural curriculum, multilingual curriculum.

KENT

Claudia Thompson
Director of Curriculum
12033 SE 256th Street
Kent, WA 98031
(206) 813-7265

Years In Operation: 6; **Grade Levels:** K-12; **Students Participating:** 24,000; **Community Participation:** community involvement in curriculum planning, use of community resources, use of human resources in the community, interaction with community organizations; **Social Goal:** single-group studies; **School Goal:** human relations; **Primary Target:** all students **Curricular Aims:** multicultural education; **Instructional Aims:** multicultural education; **School Practices:** ESL, remedial classes, culturally diverse faculty, parental involvement in school policy decisions, culturally diverse staff, community involvement in school policy decisions, strong school-community public relations effort, student involvement in school policy decisions, professionally staffed community relations office, ethnic studies curriculum; **Elements Studied:** art, attitudes, body language, culture and personality, drama, foods, history, language, literature, music, religion, social customs, social organization, social structure, values.

MUKILTEO

Marcia Migdal
Coordinator of Multicultural, Indian & International Education
20420 68th Avenue West
Lynnwood, WA 98036
(206) 670-7128

NORTHSHORE

Wynne Estes
Director, Curriculum & Student Outcomes
18315 Bothell Way NE
Bothell, WA 98011
(206) 489-6308; FAX: (206) 486-2850

Years In Operation: 5; **Grade Levels:** K-12; **Student Participation:** 18,000; **Community Participation:** use of community resources, use of human resources in the community; **Social Goal:** human relations; **School Goal:** human relations; **Primary Target:** all students; **Curricular Aims:** multicultural education; **Instructional Aims:** multicultural/social reconstructionist; **Classroom Environment:** multicultural education; **School Practices:** ESL, remedial classes, culturally diverse staff, community involvement in school policy decisions, inservice teacher training in multicultural education, human relations training for students.

Puyallup
Gwen Dewey
Director of Employment Services
109 East Pioneer
Puyallup, WA 98732
(206) 841-1301

Renton
Kay Herman
Director of Special Programs
1800 Index Avenue NE
Renton, WA 98056
(206) 204-2246

Grade Levels: K-12; **Students Participating:** 11,853; **Community Participation:** community involvement in curriculum planning, study of the community, interaction with community organizations; **Social Goal:** teaching the culturally different; **School Goal:** human relations; **Primary Target:** all students; **Curricular Aims:** multicultural education; **Instructional Aims:** multicultural education; **Classroom Environment:** multicultural/social reconstructionist; **School Practices:** ESL, remedial classes, culturally diverse faculty, parental involvement in school policy decisions, culturally diverse staff, human relations training for teachers, community involvement in school policy decisions, strong school-community public relations effort, inservice teacher training in multicultural education, student involvement in curricular planning, student involvement in school policy decisions, interracial student council, human relations training for students, professionally staffed community relations office, bilingual curriculum, ethnic studies curriculum; **Groups Studied:** African Americans, Arab Americans, Asian/Pacific Islander Americans, French Americans, German Americans, Greek Americans, Hispanic (Latino/Chicano) Americans, Iranian Americans, Irish Americans, Italian Americans, Native Americans, Portuguese Americans, Scandinavian Americans, Slavic Americans; **Elements Studied:** art, attitudes, beliefs, body language, culture and personality, dialect, drama, foods, history, kinship structure, language, literature, material culture, music, physical characteristics, religion, social customs, social organization, social structure, values; **Participating Disciplines:** language arts, social studies; **Locally Produced Materials:** yes.

SOUTH KITSAP

Kathy Klock
Curriculum Director
1962 Hoover Avenue SE
Port Orchard, WA 98366
(206) 876-7300

Years In Operation: 3; **Grade Levels:** 7-12; **Community Participation:** community involvement in curriculum planning, use of community resources, use of human resources in the community, study of the community, interaction with community organizations; **Social Goal:** human relations; **School Goal:** multicultural education; **Primary Target:** all students; **Curricular Aims:** multicultural/social reconstructionist; **Instructional Aims:** multicultural/social reconstructionist; **Classroom Environment:** multicultural education; **School Practices:** ESL, remedial classes, culturally diverse faculty, parental involvement in school policy decisions, human relations training for teachers, community involvement in school policy decisions, strong school-community public relations effort, student involvement in curricular planning, student involvement in school policy decisions.

SPOKANE

Dr. Nancy Stowell
Director of Curriculum
200 North Bernard Street
Spokane, WA 99201
(509) 455-5242

Years In Operation: 1; **Grade Levels:** K-12; **Community Participation:** use of community resources, use of human resources in the community, study of the community, interaction with community organizations; **Social Goal:** multicultural education; **School Goal:** multicultural education; **Primary Target:** all students; **Curricular Aims:** multicultural/social reconstructionist; **Instructional Aims:** multicultural education; **Classroom Environment:** multicultural education; **School Practices:** ESL, remedial classes, culturally diverse faculty, parental involvement in school policy decisions, community involvement in school policy decisions, inservice teacher training in multicultural education, professionally staffed community relations office.

TACOMA

Mimh Amh Hodge
Administrator
(206) 596-1159
Cenobio Macias
Helping Teacher
(206) 596-1140
P.O. Box 1357
Tacoma, WA 98401

Years In Operation: 20; **Grade Levels:** K-12; **Students Participating:** 1,500; **Community Participation:** use of community resources, use of human resources in the community,; **Social Goal:** human relations; **School Goal:** human relations; **Primary Target:** all students; **Curricular Aims:** human relations; **Instructional Aims:** multicultural education; **Classroom Environment:** multicultural/social reconstructionist; **School Practices:** culturally diverse faculty, strong school-community public relations effort, inservice teacher training in multicultural education, Spanish as a second language, human relations training for students, Asian language(s); **Elements Studied:** art, attitudes, beliefs, foods, literature; **Participating Disciplines:** art, foreign languages, music.

VANCOUVER

Dr. Ed Wilgus
Multicultural/Affirmative Action Resource Coordinator
605 North Devine Road
Vancouver, WA 98668-8937
(360) 696-7149; FAX: (360) 696-7027

Years In Operation: 1; **Grade Levels:** K-12; **Students Participating:** 19,000; **Community Participation:** community involvement in curriculum planning, use of community resources, use of human resources in the community, study of the community, interaction with community organizations; **Social Goal:** multicultural/social reconstructionist; **School Goal:** multicultural/social reconstructionist; **Primary Target:** all students; **Curricular Aims:** multicultural/social reconstructionist; **Instructional Aims:** multicultural/social reconstructionist; **Classroom Environment:** multicultural/social reconstructionist; **School Practices:** transitional bilingual education, ESL, culturally diverse faculty, parental involvement in school policy decisions, culturally diverse staff, human relations training for teachers, community involvement in school policy decisions, strong school-community public relations effort, inservice teacher training in multicultural education, student involvement in school policy decisions, professionally staffed community relations office, professionally staffed human relations team; **Locally Produced Materials:** yes; **Materials Available for Purchase:** yes.

Yakima
Alice Lara
104 North 4th Avenue
Yakima, WA 98902
(509) 575-3226

Years In Operation: 2; **Community Participation:** use of community resources, use of human resources in the community, study of the community, interaction with community organizations, parent advisory committee, multicultural competence committee; **Social Goal:** single-group studies; **School Goal:** multicultural education; **Primary Target:** all students; **Curricular Aims:** teaching the culturally different; **Instructional Aims:** teaching the culturally different; **Classroom Environment:** multicultural education; **School Practices:** transitional bilingual education, ESL, remedial classes, culturally diverse faculty, parental involvement in school policy decisions, culturally diverse staff, human relations training for teachers, community involvement in school policy decisions, strong school-community public relations effort, inservice teacher training in multicultural education, Spanish as a second language, human relations training for students, bilingual curriculum, bicultural curriculum, multilingual curriculum, standard English as a second dialect; **Locally Produced Materials:** yes.

WEST VIRGINIA

Berkeley County
Dr. Taylor Perry
Director of Pupil Services
401 South Queen Street
Martinsburg, WV 25401
(304) 267-3500 ext. 35

Years In Operation: 4; **Grade Levels:** K-12; **Students Participating:** 80; **Community Participation:** use of community resources, use of human resources in the community, interaction with community organizations; **Social Goal:** human relations; **School Goal:** teaching the culturally different; **Primary Target:** all students; **Curricular Aims:** multicultural education; **Instructional Aims:** human relations; **Classroom Environment:** multicultural/social reconstructionist; **School Practices:** human relations training for teachers, community involvement in school policy decisions, inservice teacher training in multicultural education, interracial student council, human relations training for students, student human relations council, multilingual curriculum.

Cabell County
Allyson Schoenlein
Curriculum Supervisor, Social Studies/Language Arts
620 20th Street
Huntington, WV 25709
(304) 528-5053

Harrison County
William Ashcraft
Assistant Superintendent
P.O. Box 1370
Clarksburg, WV 26302
(304) 624-3300

Years In Operation: 1; **Grade Levels:** 12; **Students Participating:** 25; **Community Participation:** community involvement in curriculum planning, use of community resources, use of human resources in the community, interaction with community organizations; **Social Goal:** multicultural education; **School Goal:** multicultural education; **Primary Target:** all students; **Curricular Aims:** single-group studies; **Instructional Aims:** human relations; **Classroom Environment:** multicultural/social reconstructionist; **School Practices:** ESL, remedial classes, parental involvement in school policy decisions, human relations training for teachers, inservice teacher training in multicultural education, student involvement in school policy decisions, interracial student council.

Kanawha County
Charlene H. Byrd
Assistant Superintendent/Communications & Telecommunication
200 Elizabeth Street
Charleston, WV 25311
(304) 348-7731

Monongalia
Jennifer Snyder
Assistant Superintendent
13 South High Street
Morgantown, WV 26505
(304) 291-9210 ext. 501

Wood County
James H. Bailey
Director of Staff Development, Technology & Instructional Services
1210 13th Street
Parkersburg, WV 26101
(304) 420-9633

Years In Operation: 31; **Grade Levels:** K-12; **Students Participating:** 7,000; **Community Participation:** community involvement in curriculum planning, use of community resources, use of human resources in the community, interaction with community organizations; **Social Goal:** multicultural education; **School Goal:** multicultural education; **Primary Target:** all students; **Curricular Aims:** multicultural education; **Instructional Aims:** multicultural education; **Classroom Environment:** multicultural/social reconstructionist; **School Practices:** transitional bilingual education, ESL, remedial classes, culturally diverse faculty, parental involvement in school policy decisions, culturally diverse staff, human relations training for teachers, community involvement in school policy decisions, strong school-community public relations effort, inservice teacher training in multicultural education, student involvement in curricular planning, Spanish as a second language, student involvement in school policy decisions, interracial student council, human relations training for students, ethnic studies curriculum; **Group Studied:** African Americans; **Elements Studied:** art, culture and personality, history, music, social customs, social organization, social structure; **Participating Disciplines:** social studies.

WISCONSIN

Eau Claire
Don Johnson
Director of Curriculum & Instruction
500 Main Street
Eau Claire, WI 54701
(715) 834-8104

Grade Levels: K-12; **Students Participating:** 11,000; **Community Participation:** community involvement in curriculum planning, use of community resources, use of human resources in the community, study of the community, interaction with community organizations; **Social Goal:** human relations; **School Goal:** human relations; **Primary Target:** all students; **Curricular Aims:** single-group studies; **Instructional Aims:** human relations; **Classroom Environment:** multicultural education; **School Practices:** transitional bilingual education, ESL, remedial classes, culturally diverse faculty, parental involvement in school policy decisions, human relations training for teachers, community involvement in school policy decisions, strong school-community public relations effort, inservice teacher training in multicultural education, Spanish as a second language, student involvement in school policy decisions, human relations training for students, professionally staffed community relations office, bilingual curriculum, Asian language(s); **Elements Studied:** art, attitudes, beliefs, body language, culture and personality, foods, history, kinship structure, language, literature, music, religion, social customs, social organization, social structure, values; **Locally Produced Materials:** yes.

GREEN BAY

Steve Kimball
Principal, Howe School
525 South Madison
Green Bay, WI 54301
(414) 448-2141

Years In Operation: 10; **Grade Levels:** K-12; **Students Participating:** 18,922; **Community Participation:** community involvement in curriculum planning, use of community resources, use of human resources in the community, interaction with community organizations; **Social Goal:** human relations; **School Goal:** multicultural education; **Primary Target:** all students; **Curricular Aims:** multicultural education; **Instructional Aims:** multicultural education; **Classroom Environment:** multicultural education; **School Practices:** transitional bilingual education, ESL, remedial classes, parental involvement in school policy decisions, community involvement in school policy decisions, inservice teacher training in multicultural education, Spanish as a second language, student involvement in school policy decisions, multilingual curriculum.

MADISON METROPOLITAN

Virginia M. Henderson, Ph.D.
Special Assistant to the Superintendent for Equity, Diversity, & Advocacy
545 West Dayton Street
Madison, WI 53703
(608) 266-5958

Years In Operation: 20; **Grade Levels:** K-12; **Students Participating:** 24,000; **Community Participation:** community involvement in curriculum planning, use of community resources, use of human resources in the community, a community based instructional program, interaction with community organizations; **Social Goal:** multicultural/social reconstructionist; **School Goal:** multicultural education; **Primary Target:** all students; **Curricular Aims:** multicultural/social reconstructionist; **Instructional Aims:** multicultural/social reconstructionist; **Classroom Environment:** multicultural/social reconstructionist; **School Practices:** transitional bilingual education, ESL, culturally diverse faculty, parental involvement in school policy decisions, community involvement in school policy decisions, inservice teacher training in multicultural education, Spanish as a second language, human relations training for students, professionally staffed community relations office, bilingual curriculum,professionally staffed human relations team, multilingual curriculum, Asian language(s), ethnic studies curriculum; **Groups Studied:** African Americans, Asian/

Pacific Islander Americans, Hispanic (Latino/Chicano) Americans, Native Americans; **Elements Studied:** art, beliefs, dialect, foods, history, kinship structure, language, literature, material culture, music, physical characteristics, religion, social customs, social organization, social structure, values; **Locally Produced Materials:** yes; **Materials Available for Purchase:** *Leadership Plan for Multicultural Education in the Madison Metropolitan School District.*

Milwaukee

Sharon Purtka
Staff Development Specialist, Bilingual/Multicultural Education
P.O. Box 2181
Milwaukee, WI 53201
(414) 277-4900

Years In Operation: 19; **Grade Levels:** K-12; **Students Participating:** 105,000; **Community Participation:** community involvement in curriculum planning, use of community resources, use of human resources in the community, a community based instructional program, study of the community, interaction with community organizations; **Social Goal:** multicultural education; **School Goal:** multicultural education; **Primary Target:** all students; **Curricular Aims:** multicultural education; **Instructional Aims:** multicultural/social reconstructionist; **Classroom Environment:** multicultural/social reconstructionist; **School Practices:** transitional bilingual education, ESL, remedial classes, culturally diverse faculty, parental involvement in school policy decisions, culturally diverse staff, human relations training for teachers, community involvement in school policy decisions, strong school-community public relations effort, inservice teacher training in multicultural education, student involvement in curricular planning, Spanish as a second language, student involvement in school policy decisions, interracial student council, human relations training for students, professionally staffed community relations office, bilingual curriculum, professionally staffed human relations team, student human relations council, bicultural curriculum, multilingual curriculum, standard English as a second dialect, Asian language(s), Native American language(s), ethnic studies curriculum; **Groups Studied:** African Americans, Arab Americans, Asian/Pacific Islander Americans, French Americans, German Americans, Hispanic (Latino/Chicano) Americans, Iranian Americans, Native Americans; **Elements Studied:** art, attitudes, beliefs, body language, culture and personality, dialect, drama, foods, history, kinship structure, language, literature, material culture, music, physical characteristics, religion, social customs, social organization, social structure, values; **Participating Disciplines:** art, business, English, foreign languages, health, home economics, humanities, industrial arts, language arts, mathematics, music, physical education, reading, science, social studies, theater; **Locally Produced Materials:** yes; **Materials Available for Purchase:** *Many Voices, Many Dreams* (video).

Racine

Mel Williams
Multicultural Coordinator
1012 Center Street
Racine, WI 53403
(414) 635-5865

Acknowledgments

We would like to thank the following persons who assisted in the development and production of this work: Robert W. Abbott, Andira Becker, Sam Bidleman, Deanne Ferguson, Faith G. Kline, Daniel C. Washburn, David T. Washburn, and Maria Christian Workman.

David E. Washburn is professor and coordinator of educational foundations at Bloomsburg University of Pennsylvania. He holds the B.A., M.Ed., and Ph.D. degrees from the University of Arizona and the post-doctoral certificate in multicultural education from the University of Miami. He is the author of sixteen books and monographs, including *Democracy and the Education of the Disadvantaged: A Pragmatic Inquiry*, *Ethnic Studies in Pennsylvania*, *Directory of Ethnic Studies in Pennsylvania*, *The Peoples of Pennsylvania*, *Ethnic Studies*, *Bilingual/Bicultural Education and Multicultural Teacher Education in the United States*, *The Theoretical Foundations of Teaching and Learning*, and *Multicultural Education in the United States*. Among his numerous other works are publications which have appeared in *Multicultural Education*, *Educational Foundations*, *Educational Studies* (U.S.), *Educational Studies* (England), *CORE* (England), *Phi Delta Kappan*, the *Research Bulletin* of Florida A & M University, *Pennsylvania Ethnic Studies Newsletter*, *Improving College and University Teaching*, *Minority Voices*, *Educational Leadership*, *Social Education*, *The Florida FL Reporter*, *Pennsylvania Education*, *Western Review*, *Book of Days 1987*, *America: History and Life*, and *The Journal of Global Awareness*. He has also written and produced a number of documentary films and videos, including *Dexter, Pedro, and Richard* for WTVJ Television, Miami, Florida.

Neil L. Brown is assistant professor of education at Bloomsburg University of Pennsylvania. He earned the Ed.D. in early childhood education from Temple University and conducts much of his research in the area of social studies education. The author of several texts and articles, his most recent publications include *Social Studies for Elementary Children in the 21st Century* and "Persisting and Common Stereotypes in U.S. Students' Knowledge of Africa: A Study of Preservice Social Studies Teachers" (co-author), published in *The Social Studies*.